STUDENT WORKBOOK

MATHEMATICS EXPLAINED FOR PRIMARY TEACHERS

DEREK HAYLOCK

S Sage

1 Oliver's Yard
55 City Road
London EC1Y 1SP

2455 Teller Road
Thousand Oaks
California 91320

Unit No 323-333, Third Floor, F-Block
International Trade Tower
Nehru Place, New Delhi – 110 019

8 Marina View Suite 43-053
Asia Square Tower 1
Singapore 018960

Editor: James Clark
Editorial assistant: Esosa Otabor
Assistant editor, digital: Benedict Hegarty
Production editor: Nicola Marshall
Copyeditor: Martin Noble
Proofreader: Tom Bedford
Marketing manager: Lorna Patkai
Cover design: Wendy Scott
Typeset by: C&M Digitals (P) Ltd, Chennai, India
Printed in the UK by Bell & Bain Ltd, Glasgow

Library of Congress Control Number:

British Library Cataloguing in Publication data

A catalogue record for this book is available from the British Library

ISBN 978-1-5296-2631-5 (pbk)

Contents

About the Author

Derek Haylock is an education writer, with an extensive list of publications in the field of mathematics education. He worked for over 30 years in teacher education, both initial and in-service, and was Co-Director of Primary Initial Teacher Training and responsible for the mathematics components of the primary programmes at the University of East Anglia (UEA) in Norwich. He has considerable practical experience of teaching and researching in primary classrooms. His work in mathematics education has taken him to Germany, Belgium, Lesotho, Kenya, Brunei, India and Sweden. As well as his publications in the field of education, he has written seven books of Christian drama for young people and a Christmas musical (published by Church House/National Society). For 15 years after his time at UEA, he was in great demand as a consultant and professional speaker. His work as a writer continues.

Acknowledgements

I am grateful to the primary PGCE students at the University of East Anglia (Norwich) who many years ago enthusiastically volunteered to trial some of this material prior to the first edition of this workbook and provided such encouraging and constructive feedback. Thanks also to Ralph Manning who made these trials possible and provided ideas and suggestions for the first edition. Finally, I would like to acknowledge the encouragement, support and professional guidance of James Clark of Sage Publications, along with all the team at Sage Publications who have been involved in the publication of this new edition.

The Purpose of This Workbook

This workbook provides 900 questions designed to provide the reader with a means of reviewing, reinforcing, extending, applying and reflecting on the learning and teaching of the material of *Mathematics Explained for Primary Teachers*, 7th edition (Derek Haylock, 2024, Sage Publications). The number of questions has been increased in this edition partly by including questions that relate to new material in the 7th edition of *Mathematics Explained*, particularly language and approaches consistent with the current emphasis on teaching for mastery.

Questions are provided that draw directly on the material in each of the chapters of *Mathematics Explained* that deal with mathematical knowledge, skills, concepts and principles (Chapters 6–28). So the numbering of the questions begins, unusually, with Q6.01, because the first group of questions (6.01–6.38) relate to Chapter 6 of *Mathematics Explained*.

However, Chapters 1–5 of *Mathematics Explained* are not overlooked in this workbook. Each group of questions includes examples that give an opportunity to use and develop the key processes of using and applying mathematics that are the focus of Chapters 4–5 (Section B), as well as those that relate to the principles and practice of learning and teaching primary mathematics discussed in Chapters 1–3 (Section A).

The Categories of Questions

There are three kinds of questions for you to tackle in each section of this book, although the distinctions between them are inevitably at times a little blurred.

1 Checking Understanding

These questions are designed to help you check your knowledge of terminology, your understanding of key concepts and principles, and your mastery of important skills. These questions in particular supplement the self-assessment questions in *Mathematics Explained*.

2 Reasoning and Problem Solving

These questions provide opportunities to use and apply the mathematical content of each of Chapters 6–28 of *Mathematics Explained* in order to develop the important aspects of learning mathematics outlined in Section B (Chapters 4 and 5) of the textbook. The tasks in this category provide opportunities to apply skills and knowledge in real-life situations and in mathematical puzzles, problems and investigations. These are intended to be challenging and to stretch you. The processes involved in these tasks might include, for example: communicating with mathematics; seeing and articulating patterns; making generalizations; mathematical modelling; conjecturing and hypothesizing; logical reasoning; recognizing similarities and differences; problem-solving strategies; and thinking creatively, flexibly and divergently.

3 Learning and Teaching

These questions provide opportunities to consider the content of each of Chapters 6–28 of *Mathematics Explained* in terms of approaches to learning and teaching mathematics, reflecting the principles of Section A (Chapters 1–3) of the textbook. The tasks include responses to children's errors and misunderstandings, the development of teaching ideas, the evaluation of teaching approaches, teaching for mastery and the consideration of objectives to promote understanding.

Related Chapters in *Mathematics Explained for Primary Teachers* 7th Edition

How to Use This Workbook

- You do not need to do these tasks in the order they are given.
- Don't just read the tasks. Do them! Get some paper and a pencil and engage with the material. Scribble on the pages of the workbook if necessary. Write your answers down.
- Some centimetre-squared grids are provided at the end of the book for you to use for some of the questions, such as those that involve plotting points and sketching graphs.
- If you are unsure about particular mathematical language or concepts then refer to the related chapter in *Mathematics Explained for Primary Teachers*, 7th edition, particularly the glossary provided at the end of the relevant chapter.
- You may find it helpful to work through this material with a fellow student or colleague, so that you get the opportunity to share ideas and to articulate both your difficulties and your insights.
- Detailed solutions and explanatory notes are provided at the end of the book for each task: turn to these for help only when you have really done your best to complete the task.
- Read the solutions and notes even if you have done the task successfully: they will help you to consolidate your learning.

QUESTIONS

NUMBERS AND PLACE VALUE

Questions related to Chapter 6 in *Mathematics Explained for Primary Teachers*, 7th edition.

Questions 6.01–20: Checking understanding (numbers and place value)

Question 6.01 is about a basic skill in learning to count

Q6.01:   Write down at a glance, without counting, how many x's there are below. What is this skill called?

x   x   x   x   x x

In each of **Questions 6.02–05**, match the set with one of these: natural numbers, integers, rational numbers, real numbers.

Q6.02:   The set of all numbers that can be represented by points on a continuous number line or by real lengths, including numbers like $\sqrt{2}$.

Q6.03:   {1, 2, 3, 4, 5, 6, 7, 8, 9, 10, 11, 12, ...} continuing forever.

Q6.04:   The set of all numbers – including fractions and decimals – that can be expressed as the ratio of two whole numbers.

Q6.05:   {..., –5, –4, –3, –2, –1, 0, 1, 2, 3, 4, 5, ...} continuing forever in both directions.

In each **of Questions 6.06–08**, write the numbers using place value notation; then read your answer out loud, using the correct terminology for these numbers.

Q6.06: $(4 \times 10^4) + (2 \times 10^3) + (7 \times 10) + 6$

Q6.07: $3 + (5 \times 10) + (6 \times 10^2) + (7 \times 10^6)$

Q6.08: 5×10^7

For **Questions 6.09–12** round a bill of £7099.29 …

Q6.09:   … to the nearest thousand pounds

Q6.10:   … to the nearest hundred pounds

Q6.11:   … to the nearest ten pounds

Q6.12:   … to the nearest pound.

In **Questions 6.13–15** one number is given in Hindu-Arabic numerals, the other in Roman numerals. Decide which number is nearer to 500.

Q6.13:   206 or DCCLXVIII

Q6.14:   502 or CDXCIX

Q6.15:   620 or CCCLXXVIII

Question 6.16 is about the base-ten materials shown below. A stack of 10 hundreds (flats), for example, can be replaced by a thousand block (a large cube).

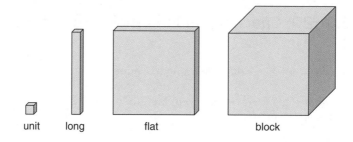

unit   long   flat   block

Q6.16:   If Tom has 9 hundreds (flats), 9 tens (longs) and 15 ones (units), what is the smallest number of pieces he can exchange these for? What nmber of units is this collection equivalent to?

Questions 6.17–20 require nothing more than counting on and back in 1s and 10s. You should not need to use a written addition or subtraction method to answer these questions, just your understanding of place value.

Q6.17:   What is the next number after 2,069,999?

Q6.18:   What number is 1 less than 4,980,000?

Q6.19:   What number is 10 more than 3,090,990?

Q6.20:   What number is 10 less than 1,500,005?

Questions 6.21-30: Reasoning and problem solving (numbers and place value)

Question 6.21 is an insignificant bit of fun with the names of counting numbers.

Q6.21: (a) Which is the only counting number that is equal to the number of letters in its name? Convince yourself there are no others. (b) Which is the only counting number that has the letters in its name in alphabetical order? Convince yourself there are no others. (c) Why would these questions not work in a French edition of this book?

Question 6.22 is about arrow cards, like those shown in Figure 6.10 in *Mathematics Explained*. To represent the whole numbers from 0 to 9, you need 10 arrow cards.

Q6.22: How many arrow cards do you need to represent the whole numbers from 0 to 99? From 0 to 999? From 0 to 9999?

Questions 6.23–26 require the application of the principles of place value to arithmetic in base eight, rather than base ten. These are some of the features of a base eight number system:

- the place value principle is 'one of these is eight of those'
- only eight digits are used: 0, 1, 2, 3, 4, 5, 6, 7
- 10 ('one zero') stands for 'eight' and 100 ('one zero zero') for 'eight eights' (sixty-four in base ten)
- counting in base eight begins like this: 1, 2, 3, 4, 5, 6, 7, 10, 11, 12, 13, 14, 15, 16, 17, 20, 21, 23, …

Q6.23: In base-eight arithmetic, what is the next number after 27? After 37? After 77? After 277?

Q6.24: The number 35 in base eight means 3 …s and 5 ones. This is equal to what number in base ten?

Q6.25: The 4-times table in base eight begins 4, 10, 14, 20, … Write down the next four numbers in this sequence. Which multiplication table in base ten has a similar pattern?

Q6.26: The 7-times table in base eight begins 7, 16, 25, … Write down the next four numbers in this sequence. Which multiplication table in base ten has a similar pattern?

Questions 6.27–30 are some problems about the early Roman numeral system. Note that in this system 4 is represented by IIII (not IV, as used later) and 9 by VIIII (not IX).

Tackling these problems will help you to appreciate the efficiency and elegance of the Hindu-Arabic place-value number system.

Q6.27: What are the three smallest (whole) numbers greater than a hundred that use fewer symbols in Roman numerals than in our place-value system?

Q6.28: What are the three smallest numbers greater than a hundred that use more symbols in Roman numerals than in our place-value system?

Q6.29: What are the three smallest numbers greater than a hundred that use the same number of symbols in Roman numerals as in our place-value system?

Q6.30: How far do you have to go before you get a sequence of 100 consecutive whole numbers that use more symbols in Roman numerals than in our place-value system?

Questions 6.31–42: Learning and teaching (numbers and place value)

Question 6.31 is about a teacher working with 3–4-year-olds, planning a display entitled 'All about 4'.

Q6.31: Bearing in mind the connections model of understanding (see Chapter 3 of *Mathematics Explained for Primary Teachers*, 7th edition) and both the cardinal and ordinal aspects of number, suggest lots of things that might go on this display.

In **Questions 6.32–34** analyse the misunderstandings shown and suggest ways of helping the child.

Q6.32: A five-year-old who can say the number that comes after 24 (25) but not the number that comes before it (23).

Q6.33: A seven-year-old who when asked to write down 'three hundred and twenty four' writes 30024.

Q6.34: A nine-year-old who when asked to add 1 to 3099 gives the answer 4000.

Question 6.35 is about a teacher-led class activity to help mastery of the concept of 'between' in relation to numbers. Three numbers less than 100 are displayed randomly on the board.

Q6.35: The numbers are 41, 39 and 60. Each child writes down which of the three numbers *lies between* the other two. How might the teacher continue the activity?

For **Questions 6.36–39**, in the light of your reading of Chapters 3 and 6 of *Mathematics Explained*, consider what a child should actually be able to do to show some level of mastery of the concept of place value. To do this, you are asked to write some examples of specific learning objectives for understanding this principle in terms of whole numbers. Objectives should be written to follow the phrase, 'The child should be able to …'

Q6.36: State two objectives that focus on the principle of exchange ('one of these is ten of those').

Q6.37: State two objectives that focus on the connections between symbols, language and concrete materials.

Q6.38: State two objectives that focus on the connections between the number line and the language and symbols of number.

Q6.39: State two objectives that focus on the process of putting numbers in order.

Questions 6.40–42 are about a small-group game called Boxes. Each player has a calculator and a strip with six empty boxes, as shown below. These will eventually be filled with single digits, to make an addition of two three-digit numbers. In turn, each player turns over a card from a pack of cards on which are written single digits. This card can be placed in any empty box on one of the strips, either one of the player's own boxes or one of the boxes of another player. This continues until all the boxes are full. Then the calculators are used to do the additions (so the children do not spend too much time on calculations, but focus on the principles of place value). The highest total is the winner of that round. Play ten rounds, writing down the scores for each round, and then find the overall winner by adding up all ten scores for each player.

Q6.40: What strategies might a player use in this game?

Q6.41: How might this game help to develop understanding of place value?

Q6.42: Make up a version using subtraction, avoiding negative scores.

| ADDITION AND SUBTRACTION STRUCTURES |

Questions related to Chapter 7 in *Mathematics Explained for Primary Teachers*, 7th edition.

Questions 7.1–15: Checking understanding (addition and subtraction structures)

Question 7.01 is simply to check your knowledge of some technical words in addition and subtraction.

Q7.01:   One word in each of the following statements is incorrect. Identify it and say what should the word be?

(a) 23 × (27 – 8) is a difficult sum. (b) In the calculation 17 + 12 = 29, the 17 and the 12 are adenoids and the 29 is their sum. (c) In the calculation 25 – 19 = 6, the 25 is the minuet, the 19 is the subtrahend and the 6 is the difference between 25 and 19.

Questions 7.02–03 are simply to check your understanding of the terminology 'discrete sets' and 'the union of two sets'.

Q7.02:   For (a), (b) and (c), are the two sets discrete?

a   The set of children in Year 2 and the set of six-year-olds in Year 2.

b   The set of six-year-olds in Year 2 and the set of seven-year-olds in Year 2.

c   The set of letters in the word *junior* and the set of letters in the word *secondary*.

Q7.03:   There are 6 letters used in the word *junior* and 9 letters in the word *secondary*. How many letters in the union of these two sets?

For each of **Questions 7.04–09**, make up a problem corresponding to the given addition or subtraction using the structure and context stated.

Q7.04:   The addition, 250 + 125, using the aggregation structure and liquid volume in the context of cooking.

Q7.05:   The addition, 15 + 40, using the augmentation structure in the context of age.

Q7.06:   The subtraction, 25 – (–6), using the comparison structure in the context of temperatures.

Q7.07: The subtraction, 7.30 – 2.50, using the reduction structure in the context of shopping.

Q7.08: The subtraction, 286 – 196, using the inverse-of-addition structure in the context of sport.

Q7.09: The subtraction, 24 – 19, using the comparison structure in the context of sport.

Questions 7.10–12 are about recognizing various subtraction structures.

Q7.10: An important event is planned for 1 January 2061. On 1 January 2026 how many years are there to wait? What subtraction calculation is required to answer this? Of what subtraction structure is this an example?

Q7.11: Jack's pail of water weighs 6450 grams and Jill's weighs 8135 grams. How much heavier is Jill's? What subtraction calculation is required to answer this? Of what subtraction structure is this an example?

Q7.12: Joe takes 55 grams of butter from a 250-gram pack to make some biscuits. How much butter is left in the pack? What subtraction calculation is required to answer this? Of what subtraction structure is this an example?

For **Questions 7.13–15** decide how you would show the calculation 92 – 67 on the number line provided below, using different interpretations of the subtraction.

0   92

Q7.13: How would you show the subtraction as 'reducing 92 by 67'?

Q7.14: How would you show the subtraction as 'comparing 92 and 67 and finding the difference'?

Q7.15: How would you show the subtraction as 'adding something to 67 to get to 92'?

Questions 7.16–24: Reasoning and problem solving (addition and subtraction structures)

Questions 7.16–17 are two more examples of recognizing subtraction structures in real-life contexts.

Q7.16: I have saved £578 but I need £765 to buy a new bicycle. What calculation would I enter on my calculator to work out how much more I need? Which subtraction structure is being used here?

Q7.17: The attendance at the Manchester United football match is 32,457. On the same day, at the Norwich City match the attendance is 14,589. Use a calculator to compare these two figures and write down three different sentences in English to express the comparison.

Questions 7.18–24 provide some word problems that are deliberately contrived to use different structures for addition or subtraction from those discussed in Chapter 7 of *Mathematics Explained for Primary Teachers*, as well as potentially misleading language. Identify the key mathematical language used in each of these. Decide whether the two numbers in each problem have to be added or subtracted, and write down the answer to the question.

Q7.18: Ralph spent £3.49 of his cash this afternoon and now he has £12.27 left. How much cash did he have this morning?

Q7.19: Martin earned £13.40 today. When this is added to his earnings so far this month, he has earned £127.25 altogether. How much had he earned before today?

Q7.20: Derek wins 29 of Anne's marbles and now she has only 37 left. How many marbles did Anne have to begin with?

Q7.21: Suzy has 349 stamps in her collection and this is 137 more than Gill has in hers. How many stamps does Gill have?

Q7.22: Suzy's suitcase weighs 27.8 kg and this is 4.7 kg less than Gill's. What does Gill's suitcase weigh?

Q7.23: Model A costs £128 more than Model B and £365 more than Model C. How much more expensive than Model B is Model C?

Q7.24: Model A costs £128 more than model B and £365 less than Model C. What is the difference in the costs of Model B and Model C?

Questions 7.25–44: Learning and teaching (addition and subtraction structures)

Question 7.25 is about the transition from 'counting all' to 'counting on' in the development of young children's understanding of addition. 'Counting all' for 5 + 3: the child counts 5 fingers on one hand and continues with 3 more on the other, so counts from 1 to 8. 'Counting on': the child puts up 5 fingers on one hand and continues counting on the other … 6, 7, 8.

Q7.25: Suggest some ways in which you could help young children to move on from 'counting all' to 'counting on'.

In **Question 7.26**, a teacher has written the three numbers 6, 8 and 14 on the board for a class of 6–7-year-olds. The first two questions the teacher asks are: 'What is 6 add 8?' and 'What is 14 subtract 8?' The teacher then proceeds with a question-and-answer session based on the relationship between these three numbers.

Q7.26:   Using a range of addition and subtraction structures, a variety of language and a range of contexts, suggest ten further questions that could be asked, using two of these numbers in the question with the other number in the answer. Example: 'If I have £14 and I pay £6 for parking my car, how much do I have left?'

Questions 7.27–33 provide examples of stories written by children aged 7–8 years to go with the addition 28 + 16, in various contexts suggested by the teacher. Check whether these are correct interpretations of 28 + 16 and identify what structure of addition is being used.

Q7.27:   I spent £28 on some trainers and £16 on a football. How much did I spend altogether?

Q7.28:   The bucket contained 28 cupfuls of water; then we poured in 16 more cupfuls. How much water is now in the bucket?

Q7.29:   In a class there are 28 girls and 16 boys. How many children are there?

Q7.30:   A boy had 28 sweets and his friend had only 16 sweets. So they shared them. How many did they have?

Q7.31:   John baked 28 cakes. His sister baked 16. How many cakes did they bake altogether?

Q7.32:   The chocolate bar was 28p last week, but today the price increased by 16p. What does it cost now?

Q7.33:   The plant was 28 cm tall. It has grown another 16 cm. How tall is it now?

Questions 7.34–40 provide examples of stories written by children aged 8–9 years to go with the subtraction 28 − 16, in various contexts suggested by the teacher. Check whether these are correct interpretations of 28 − 16 and identify what structure of subtraction is being used.

Q7.34:   There are 28 trees in a forest and an elephant knocks over 16 of them. How many trees are left standing?

Q7.35:   We had 28 kg of potatoes, but we have eaten 16 kg of them. How many kilograms are left?

Q7.36:   My friend is 28 and his brother is 16. How much older than his brother is my friend?

Q7.37:   There were 28 workers but 16 were ill. How many were not ill?

Q7.38:   The price of a chocolate bar was 28p. The shop thought it was dear and took 16p off. How much does it cost now?

Q7.39:   My friend has 28 marbles and this is 16 less than me. How many marbles have I got?

Q7.40:   Monika is 16 years old. How many years until she is 28 years old?

Questions 7.41–42 are two examples of errors that can be made by children by using an inappropriate process for addition or subtraction. Think about the structures for addition and subtraction that are involved here.

Q7.41:   A six-year-old counting on using a number line to do additions consistently gets answers 1 less than the correct answer. Why might this be? How might you help this child?

Q7.42:   A seven-year-old counting back using a number line to do subtractions consistently gets answers 1 less than the correct answer. Why might this be? How might you help this child?

Questions 7.43–44 refer to bar-modelling. See Figure 7.9 in *Mathematics Explained for Primary Teachers*, 7th edition.

Q7.43:   Refer to Q7.21 above. How might this problem be represented and solved using bar-modelling. Where in the bar-model is the answer represented?

Q7.44:   Refer to Q7.22 above. How might this problem be represented and solved using bar-modelling. Where in the bar-model is the answer represented?

MENTAL STRATEGIES FOR ADDITION AND SUBTRACTION

Questions related to Chapter 8 in *Mathematics Explained for Primary Teachers*, 7th edition.

Questions 8.01–16: Checking understanding (mental strategies for addition and subtraction)

For each statement in **Questions 8.01–05**, decide whether or not it is true for all values of p.

Q8.01: $25 + p = p + 25$

Q8.02: $8 + (25 + p) = (25 + 8) + p$

Q8.03: $25 - (p - 8) = (25 - p) - 8$

Q8.04: $25 - p - 8 = (25 - 8) - p$

Q8.05: $25 - (8 + p) = (25 - p) + 8$

In **Questions 8.06–09** fill in the missing words.

Q8.06:   The .... law of addition allows you to change $3 + 79$ to $79 + 3$.

Q8.07:   The .... law of addition allows you to change $(7 + 36) + 14$ to $7 + (36 + 14)$.

Q8.08:   The numbers 20, 90, 200 and 360 are all .... of 10.

Q8.09:   Two helpful images for supporting mental calculation processes are the .... square and the .... number line.

In **Questions 8.10–16** use the suggested mental strategy for each of the additions or subtractions.

Q8.10:   Calculate $386 + 243$ using partitioning into hundreds, tens and ones, and a front-end approach.

Q8.11:   Calculate $247 + 245$, using near-doubles.

Q8.12:   Calculate $287 - 144$, using near-doubles.

Q8.13:   Calculate $734 - 629$ by relating it to a different calculation with a friendlier number than 734.

Q8.14:   Calculate $513 - 198$ using compensation. Show your method on an empty number line.

Q8.15:   Calculate $924 - 678$ by adding on from 678 and using 680, 700 and 900 as stepping stones. Show your method on an empty number line.

Q8.16:   Calculate $1098 + 6$, by counting on.

Questions 8.17-28: Reasoning and problem solving (mental strategies for addition and subtraction)

Question 8.17 is a little discovery that may amuse you, but (hint!) it will work only in the English language.

Q8.17:   In what way are 'TWELVE ADD ONE' and 'ELEVEN ADD TWO' the same, apart from giving the same answer?

In **Questions 8.18–21** put addition or subtraction signs in the boxes to make the statements correct.

Q8.18: $892 - 566 = 892 - (600 - 34) = 892 \; \square \; 600 \; \square \; 34$

Q8.19: $892 - 566 = 892 - (500 + 66) = 892 \; \square \; 500 \; \square \; 66$

Q8.20: $892 - 566 = (900 - 8) - (600 - 34) = 900 \; \square \; 600 \; \square \; 34 \; \square \; 8$

Q8.21: $892 - 566 = (900 - 8) - (500 + 66) = 900 \; \square \; 500 \; \square \; 66 \; \square \; 8$

Questions 8.22–23 are to be answered – as I hope you would in a real-life context – by doing the calculations mentally, using whatever informal methods you consider most appropriate.

Q8.22:   What is the difference in price between two builders' estimates of £7365 and £5879 respectively?

Q8.23:   What is the total cost of two computers costing £496 and £377 respectively? How far short is this of a total budget of £1000?

Question 8.24 is a little mathematical curiosity, giving you an opportunity to apply your mental calculation skills. It involves five steps.

Step 1:   Write down a three-digit number with different first and last digits (for example, 753).

Step 2:   Now write it down again with the digits reversed (for example, 357).

Step 3:   Mentally, find the difference between the two numbers you have written down. (If this is a two-digit answer, then make it three-digit by writing zero in the hundreds place.)

Step 4:   Now write down this difference (in my example, 396) and write it down again with the digits reversed (693).

Step 5:   Mentally, find the sum of these two numbers.

Q8.24:   Follow the five steps given, using a different number. With my example I get 1089. What do you get? Try this with several different starting numbers. Intrigued?

Questions 8.25–28 are about the knight's move in chess, which is 2 units in one direction and 1 unit in the other. For example, 2 steps up and 1 to the right, 2 to the left and 1 down and so on. This question has a great deal of data to be organized and therefore requires a very systematic approach. Think about how best to organize the data.

Q8.25:   Starting at 55 on a hundred square, what are the numbers of the eight squares you can reach with a knight's move?

Q8.26:　To what additions or subtractions do the moves in Question 8.25 correspond?

Q8.27:　How many different squares can you reach from 55 using *two* knight's moves?

Q8.28:　To what additions or subtractions do each of the pairs of moves in Question 8.27 correspond?

Questions 8.29–45: Learning and teaching (mental strategies for addition and subtraction)

Questions 8.29–30 refer to ten-frames as shown in Figure 8.7 in *Mathematics Explained for Primary Teachers,* 7th edition. A teacher is using these to help some younger children to extend their skills in addition and subtraction.

Q8.29:　Suggest two ways in which children might use ten-frames for the calculation 8 + 6.

Q8.30:　Suggest two ways in which children might use ten-frames for the calculation 13 – 8.

Questions 8.31–33 are about calculating 1000 – 236 mentally.

Q8.31:　Use a mental method to find the answer to this subtraction.

Q8.32:　A ten-year-old child gets the answer 874. How does this common error in subtraction occur?

Q8.33:　How would you help this child to recognize the error here and to learn from it?

In **Questions 8.34–40** decide how you might help children to understand important calculation strategies by using a hundred square for the given calculations.

Q8.34:　37 + 21

Q8.35:　96 – 43

Q8.36:　8 + 57

Q8.37:　37 + 16

Q8.38:　43 – 17

Q8.39:　55 + 19

Q8.40:　55 – 19

In **Questions 8.41–44** identify the most likely errors in reasoning in the incorrect calculations produced by some ten-year-olds. Suggest how you would help children to recognize and learn from these errors.

Q8.41:   296 + 142 = 3138

Q8.42:   375 − 184 = 211

Q8.43:   703 − 482 = 381

Q8.44:   573 − 239 = 332

For **Question 8.45**, a teacher has some weighing scales, with two pans, A and B, and a supply of 100-gram, 10-gram and 1-gram masses (weights).

Q8.45:   How would the teacher use this equipment to explain how to find the difference between 306 and 124 by adding on?

WRITTEN METHODS FOR ADDITION AND SUBTRACTION

Questions related to Chapter 9 in *Mathematics Explained for Primary Teachers*, 7th edition.

Questions 9.01–10: Checking understanding (written methods for addition and subtraction)

Questions 9.01–05 are addition and subtraction calculations using different layouts.

Q9.01:   Fill in the missing numbers in this calculation of 6572 + 1619.

$$6000 + 500 + 70 + 2$$
$$+\ 1000 + \boxed{} + \boxed{} + 9$$
$$\overline{7000 + \boxed{} + \boxed{} + \boxed{} = \boxed{}}$$

Q9.02:   Fill in the missing numbers in this calculation of 6572 + 1619.

$$
\begin{array}{r}
6572 \\
+\ 1619 \\
\end{array}
$$

6000 + 1000 = ☐

500 + 600 = ☐

70 + ☐ = ☐

☐ + ☐ = ☐

☐

Q9.03:   Fill in the missing numbers in this calculation of 6572 + 1619.

$$
\begin{array}{r}
6\ 5\ 7\ 2 \\
+\ 1\ 6\ 1\ 9 \\
\hline
\boxed{} \\
\hline
1\quad 1
\end{array}
$$

Q9.04:   Fill in the missing numbers in this calculation of 6572 − 1619.

☐   ☐

6000 + 1500 + 70 + 12

−[1000 + ☐ + ☐ + 9]

4000 + ☐ + ☐ + ☐ = ☐

Q9.05:   Fill in the missing numbers in this calculation of 6572 − 1619.

$$
\begin{array}{r}
\boxed{}\ \ 6 \\
6\ {}^{15}5\ \not7\ {}^{1}2 \\
-\ 1\ 6\ 1\ 9 \\
\hline
\boxed{} \\
\end{array}
$$

Use **Questions 9.06–07** to practise the constant difference method of subtraction.

Q9.06:   Complete the following steps in doing a subtraction using the constant difference method.

8274 − 1496 = (   ) − 1500

= (   ) − 2000

= (   )

Q9.07:   Do the subtraction 7021 − 2893 in a similar way.

Do the subtractions in **Questions 9.08–10** using the formal written method of decomposition. These are tricky because of the zeros in the first number. Check your results by doing an addition.

Q9.08:   703 – 498

Q9.09:   4006 – 278

Q9.10:   20,005 – 12,345

Questions 9.11–17: Reasoning and problem solving (written methods for addition and subtraction)

Question Q9.11 is a challenging problem requiring some creative mathematical reasoning!

Q9.11:   The letters in the addition and subtraction calculations with four-digit numbers given below represent different digits. Any letter that appears in both calculations represents the same digit. Find the values of the digits, A, B, C, D, E and F.

$$
\begin{array}{r}
\text{E A C A} \\
+ \text{\underline{C A B 7}} \\
\text{A D 7 6}
\end{array}
\qquad
\begin{array}{r}
\text{D D B C} \\
- \text{\underline{B F E D}} \\
\text{7 7 7 7}
\end{array}
$$

Questions 9.12–17 provide an opportunity to compare informal calculation methods with formal written algorithms in calculations that arise in real-life contexts.

Q9.12:   What is the difference in price between two builders' estimates of £7365 and £5879 respectively? Use a formal, written subtraction algorithm to answer this question. What addition would you do to check your answer?

Q9.13:   Use a formal, written addition method to find the total cost of two computers costing £496 and £377 respectively. Use a formal, written subtraction method to find how far short this is of a total budget of £1000.

Q9.14:   Questions 9.12 and 9.13 are the same as Questions 8.22 and 8.23, where you were asked to do the calculations by informal methods. Which methods did you find most appropriate for these questions – the informal methods used in those questions or the formal algorithms used here?

Q9.15:   The attendances at two FA Cup semi-final football matches are reported as 27,856 and 31,258. Calculate the total attendance at the two matches, using (a) a formal written algorithm for addition, and (b) an informal addition strategy.

Q9.16: For the matches in Question 9.15, calculate the difference in attendance, using (a) a formal written algorithm for subtraction, and (b) an informal subtraction strategy.

Q9.17: In Questions 9.15 and 9.16, which method did you find most appropriate – (a) or (b)?

Questions 9.18–26: Learning and teaching (written methods for addition and subtraction)

In **Questions 9.18–21** correct and comment on the errors in the calculations.

Q9.18:
$$\begin{array}{r} 7\,1\,4\,2 \\ +\ \ 2\,9\,0\,0 \\ \hline 9\,1\,0\,4\,2 \\ \hline \end{array}$$

Q9.19:
$$\begin{array}{r} 4\,0\,2\,8 \\ +\ \ \ \,6\,2\,8 \\ \hline 1\,0\,3\,0\,8 \\ \hline \end{array}$$

Q9.20:
$$\begin{array}{r} 2\,0\,8\,4 \\ -\ \ 1\,3\,3\,9 \\ \hline 1\,3\,5\,5 \\ \hline \end{array}$$

Q9.21:
$$\begin{array}{r} 6\,5\,6^{1}3 \\ -\ 3\,4\,5\,6 \\ \hline 3\,1\,1\,7 \\ \hline \end{array}$$

Questions 9.22–25 are about helping children to connect the formal processes of addition and subtraction calculations with the manipulation of base-ten blocks (hundreds, tens and units).

Q9.22: Write a series of questions that a teacher might ask to help children understand the addition 53 + 37, by connecting the process with the manipulation of base-ten blocks (tens and units). The first two questions might be:

How do we say this first number (pointing to the numeral 53)?

How can we show this number using these tens and unit blocks?

Q9.23:   Do the same as in Question 9.22 for the subtraction 72 – 48. The first two questions might be:

How do we say this first number (pointing to the numeral 72)?

How can we show this number using these tens and unit blocks?

Q9.24:   Write a series of questions that a teacher might ask to help children understand the addition 469 + 372, by connecting the process with the manipulation of base-ten blocks (hundreds, tens and units). The first two questions might be:

How do we say this first number (pointing to the numeral 469)?

How can we show this number using these hundreds, tens and unit blocks?

Q9.25:   Do the same as in Question 9.24 for the subtraction 628 – 473. The first two questions might be:

How do we say this first number (pointing to the numeral 628)?

How can we show this number using these hundreds, tens and unit blocks?

Question 9.26 is about teaching subtraction using the method of decomposition.

Q9.26:   Make a list of some key principles to reinforce when teaching for mastery of the method of decomposition for subtraction with three-digit numbers.

MULTIPLICATION AND DIVISION STRUCTURES

Questions related to Chapter 10 in *Mathematics Explained for Primary Teachers*, 7th edition.

Questions 10.01–09: Checking understanding (multiplication and division structures)

Questions 10.01–05 are for you to check your understanding of some basic vocabulary. Fill in the missing words.

Q10.01:   When 5 is multiplied by 7 to get the answer 35, 5 is called the *multiplicand*, 7 is the ...... and 35 is the ...... of 5 and 7.

Q10.02:   A price of £75 is 3 times a price of £25. The 3 is the ...... of 75 to 25.

Q10.03: A three-letter word meaning 'for each' is ....

Q10.04: If a page of 21 cm in length is enlarged on a photocopier so that it is now 42 cm in length, it has been ...... by a ...... of 2.

Q10.05: 28 divided by 3 is 9, with a .... of 1.

Questions 10.06–07 relate to the rectangular array of counters shown below.

Q10.06: What four statements involving multiplication or division might this represent?

Q10.07: What important property of multiplication does this array demonstrate?

For each of **Questions 10.08–09**, invent three different stories that correspond to the given multiplication or division, using a variety of contexts and key language, and different structures.

Q10.08: Write stories for the multiplication 6 × 15 = 90.

Q10.09: Write stories for the division 60 ÷ 12 = 5.

Questions 10.10-24: Reasoning and problem solving (multiplication and division structures)

In **Questions 10.10–15** each of a and b stands for any number greater than or equal to zero. To answer these questions, it may help to try various values for a and b.

Q10.10: If $a \div b$ equals 3, what is the value of $b \div a$?

Q10.11: When is $a \div b$ less than $b \div a$?

Q10.12: When is $a \div b$ greater than 1?

Q10.13: When is $a \div b$ equal to zero?

Q10.14: If $a \div b$ equals zero, what can you say about $b \div a$?

Q10.15: When we say that division is not commutative, we mean that, in general, $a \div b$ is not equal to $b \div a$. But when does $a \div b$ equal $b \div a$?

Question 10.16 is about a well-known bogus proof that 1 = 2.

Q10.16: What is wrong with this 'proof' that 1 = 2?

We know that $1 \times 0 = 0$ and $2 \times 0 = 0$

Therefore, $1 \times 0 = 2 \times 0$.

Divide both sides by zero.

Therefore, 1 = 2.

Questions 10.17–22 use the idea of multiplication as scaling and division as ratio. Ann and Ben currently earn £60 an hour and £20 an hour respectively.

Q10.17: How many times greater is Ann's hourly pay than Ben's?

Q10.18: What is the *ratio* of Ann's hourly pay to Ben's?

Q10.19: Both rates of pay are scaled up by the same factor. Does the ratio of Ann's hourly pay to Ben's increase, decrease or stay the same?

Q10.20: Both rates of pay are scaled down by the same factor. Does the ratio of Ann's hourly pay to Ben's increase, decrease or stay the same?

Q10.21: Both rates of pay are increased by the same amount. Does the ratio of Ann's hourly pay to Ben's increase, decrease or stay the same?

Q10.22: Both rates of pay are decreased by the same amount. Does the ratio of Ann's hourly pay to Ben's increase, decrease or stay the same?

In **Questions 10.23–24** Jo and Jack get the same pocket money each month; it is a multiple of £1.50.

Q10.23: Which of the following could not be the monthly pocket money they each receive: £3, £4.50, £5, £7.50, £9, £12.50?

Q10.24: One month Jo spent all her pocket money on toys costing 50p per toy. The next month she spent it all on toys costing £1 per toy. Jack spent all his pocket money for these two months on toys costing 75p per toy. Who got the most toys? Or did they get the same number?

Questions 10.25–33: Learning and teaching (multiplication and division structures)

For **Questions 10.25–28** imagine that you, the teacher, have written on the board the multiplication statement, $6 \times 9 = 54$. You now pose a series of multiplication and division questions to the class, using the relationship between the three numbers involved in this multiplication.

Q10.25:   Make up a multiplication question about envelopes that cost 6p each.

Q10.26:   Make up a division question about envelopes that cost 6p each.

Q10.27:   Make up a question that compares nine-year-old Jack's age with that of his granny.

Q10.28:   Now make up another ten questions that use the relationship between the numbers 6, 9 and 54, using a range of multiplication and division language, structures and contexts. Include some context-free questions.

Question 10.29 is about a teacher with a class of children aged 7–8 years.

Q10.29:   The teacher brings in a supply of plant pots and a rectangular tray designed to hold 5 rows of 6 pots. How could these resources be used effectively to develop key multiplication and division language and concepts?

For **Questions 10.30–33** suggest how you would demonstrate the given mathematical ideas on a number line.

Q10.30:   The commutativity of multiplication?

Q10.31:   Multiplication by zero?

Q10.32:   Division as the inverse of multiplication?

Q10.33:   Division by zero is not possible.

MENTAL STRATEGIES FOR MULTIPLICATION AND DIVISION

Questions related to Chapter 11 in *Mathematics Explained for Primary Teachers*, 7th edition.

Questions 11.01–10: Checking understanding (mental strategies for multiplication and division)

For each of **Questions 11.01–02**, make up a division problem in a real-life context.

Q11.01:   … in which 24 is the dividend and 2 is the divisor.

Q11.02:   … in which 2 is the quotient and 12 is the divisor.

Do the calculations in **Questions 11.03–07** by mental strategies, using the given starting point:

Q11.03: 23×19 (use $19 = 20 - 1$)

Q11.04: 41×23 (use $23 = 1 + 2 + 4 + 16$ and doubling)

Q11.05: $408 \div 24$ (use $10 \times 24 = 240$, $5 \times 24 = 120$, …)

Q11.06: $408 \div 24$ (divide both numbers by 2 to get an equivalent ratio)

Q11.07: $319 \div 11$ (write 319 as $99 + \ldots$)

In **Questions 11.08–10** identify the mathematical laws used in the calculation.

Q11.08: $425 \times 18 = (425 \times 20) - (425 \times 2)$

Q11.09: $25 \times 48 = 25 \times (4 \times 12) = (25 \times 4) \times 12$

Q11.10: $168 \div 4 = (160 \div 4) + (8 \div 4)$

Questions 11.11-21: Reasoning and problem solving (mental strategies for multiplication and division)

Questions 11.11–14 are about using one multiplication result to deduce other multiplication or division results without doing any difficult calculations. Assume you are given that $56 \times 84 = 4704$.

Q11.11:   Write down the value of 84×56.

Q11.12:   Write down the value of 560×84.

Q11.13:   Write down seven other multiplication results that you can deduce from the given result.

Q11.14:   Write down four division results that you can deduce from the given result.

Do all the calculations in **Questions 11.15–18** mentally.

Q11.15:   Find 9×11, 19×21, 29×31, 39×41 and 49×51.

Q11.16:   Articulate a generalization from the above results.

Q11.17:   Use the generalization to calculate 199×201.

Q11.18:   If $37 \times 37 = 1369$, what is 36×38?

Try to answer each of **Questions 11.19–21** within 30 seconds of reading the question! Do not write anything down.

Q11.19: I have just completed a 1000-piece jigsaw that is a picture of 24 different kinds of bees. There were 144 of something that made this tricky. 144 what?

Q11.20: Coaches seat 75 passengers. How many coaches would you need for 600 passengers?

Q11.21: A shop offers a TV for £480 or 24 monthly payments of £25.25. How much extra do you pay if you go for the monthly instalments?

Questions 11.22–38: Learning and teaching (mental strategies for multiplication and division)

For **Questions 11.22–25** suggest how you would help some children aged 10–11 years to approach the multiplication 75×12 using the strategy indicated.

Q11.22: By thinking of the 12 as $2 \times 2 \times 3$.

Q11.23: By thinking of the 12 as $10 + 2$.

Q11.24: By thinking of the 75 as $64 + 8 + 2 + 1$.

Q11.25: By thinking of the 75 as $50 + 25$.

For **Questions 11.26–27** some children are calculating how many tiles in total are needed to tile a bathroom wall with 13 rows of 37 square tiles.

Q11.26: Suggest how the calculation might be done using relationships suggested by the rectangular array of tiles.

Q11.27: The teacher then asks how we might use the answer to this question to work out how many tiles would be needed for 13 rows of 38 tiles. A child replies 482. Identify the error here and suggest how to use this situation to promote learning.

For **Questions 11.28–31** a teacher has 15 boxes of coloured pencils: 6 blue and 6 red in each box. The class is discussing the multiplication 15×12. How could the teacher use the boxes of pencils to illustrate the four different ways suggested for approaching this calculation mentally?

Q11.28: $15 \times 12 = (10 \times 12) + (5 \times 12)$

Q11.29: $15 \times 12 = (5 \times 12) \times 3$

Q11.30: $15 \times 12 = (15 \times 6) + (15 \times 6)$

Q11.31: $15 \times 12 = (15 \times 10) + (15 \times 2)$

Questions 11.32–35 are examples of a simplified version of the number round in the Channel 4 TV programme, *Countdown*. These provide good problem-solving experience for older primary school children. Try these yourself and make up some more rounds you could use with children you might be teaching. Any of the four operations, addition, subtraction, multiplication and division, can be used in any order.

Q11.32:   Use these three numbers: 7, 25 and 3. How would you get the answer 100?

Q11.33:   Use these four numbers: 6, 7, 8 and 9. How would you get the answer 59?

Q11.34:   Use these four numbers: 13, 63, 7 and 8. How would you get the answer 45?

Q11.35:   Some children will enjoy doing the full *Countdown* number round. Here's an example for you to try. Numbers available: 7, 2, 9, 1, 75. Target: 543.

Question 11.36 reveals an intriguing fact that might help some children to remember one of the more difficult results in the multiplication tables.

Q11.36:   Here's a simple multiplication fact: $12 = 3 \times 4$. Notice how the digits 1, 2, 3, 4 appear in order in this result. Can you find another multiplication result like this?

Questions 11.37–38 are about helping children to use bar-modelling to identify the calculation required in a two-step mathematical problem.

Q11.37:   On a bookshelf there are 60 books, fiction and non-fiction. The number of fiction books is 4 times the number of non-fiction. How many non-fiction are there?

Q11.38:   How might you use bar-modelling to help children to avoid the trap of dividing 60 by 4 to get the answer 15 to the question in 11.37?

WRITTEN METHODS FOR MULTIPLICATION AND DIVISION

Questions related to Chapter 12 in *Mathematics Explained for Primary Teachers*, 7th edition.

Questions 12.01–10: Checking understanding (written methods for multiplication and division)

Questions 12.01–03 are about the long multiplication algorithm used to calculate 139×24.

$$
\begin{array}{r}
139 \\
\times \quad 24 \\
\hline
2780 \\
556 \\
\hline
3336 \\
\hline
\end{array}
$$

Q12.01: What specific calculation produces the number 2780 in the above format?

Q12.02: What specific calculation produces the number 556?

Q12.03: What specific calculation produces the number 3336?

Questions 12.04–06 are also about the written calculation of 139 × 24, but done in a less compact form.

$$
\begin{array}{r}
139 \\
\times \quad 24 \\
\hline
2000 \\
600 \\
180 \\
400 \\
120 \\
36 \\
\hline
3336 \\
\hline
\end{array}
$$

Q12.04: What specific calculations produce the numbers 2000, 600 and 180 in the above format?

Q12.05: What specific calculations produce the numbers 120, 36 and 3336?

Q12.06: Draw a rectangle divided into six smaller rectangles to represent the six multiplications involved in the calculation in Questions 12.04 and 12.05.

Questions 12.07–10 are about different written methods for division calculations.

Q12.07: Here is a calculation of 259 ÷ 7 done by the method of short division. Explain where the little 4 in front of the 9 comes from and what it represents.

$$
\begin{array}{r}
3\ 7 \\
\hline
7\ \big)\ 2\ 5\,^{4}9 \\
\end{array}
$$

Q12.08: Fill in the missing numbers in this calculation of 478 ÷ 28 using the ad hoc subtraction method.

$$478 \div 28$$

```
        | 478 ÷ 28
  10    | 280
        | [   ]
  [  ]  | 140
        | [   ]
   2    |  56
  [  ] [   ]  remainder
```

Q12.09: Fill in the missing numbers in this calculation of $458 \div 28$ using the long division method.

```
        1 6 remainder 10
  28 | 4 5 8
       □↓
       ─────
       1 7 8
       □
       □
```

Q12.10: In this long division calculation, the dividend and the divisor have been hidden. What are they?

```
              4 9 remainder 28
  □ | □
      1 6 8
      4 0 6
      3 7 8
        2 8
```

Questions 12.11–21 Reasoning and problem solving (written methods for multiplication and division)

Questions 12.11–12 provide a long multiplication calculation and a short division calculation in which the letters A, B, C, D, P and Q represent various digits. Your challenge is to work out what they must be!

Q12.11: Suggestion: start by deciding what the value of A must be.

$$
\begin{array}{r}
2\,\text{A}6 \\
\times\ \ \ 3\,\text{B} \\
\hline
6\Delta\text{XA} \\
\text{X}2\,\text{B} \\
\hline
7\text{AAB}
\end{array}
$$

Q12.12: Suggestion: start by considering various possibilities for the value of P.

$$
\begin{array}{r}
\text{Q Q Q Q} \\
\text{P}\,\overline{)\,7\ \text{P}\ \ \text{P}\ \ \text{P}\ \ 2\,}
\end{array}
$$

Use written calculation methods to answer **Questions 12.13–15.**

Q12.13: What is the cost of employing 17 bricklayers at £23 per hour for 35 hours?

Q12.14: How many teachers are needed for a school of 778 children, to meet their target of a staffing ratio of 1 teacher to 23 children?

Q12.15: A chicken farmer uses egg trays that hold 36 eggs each. How many egg trays can the farmer fill with the 500 eggs collected one morning?

Questions 12.16–21 explore further the idea of using areas of rectangles to understand multiplication.

Q12.16: Use this area diagram to calculate 74 × 3.

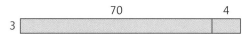

Q12.17: Use the result of Question 12.16 to work out 74 × 6, 74 × 9 and 74 × 12.

Q12.18: The area method can be used by partitioning the numbers into hundreds, tens and ones. For example, because you now know 74 × 6 and 74 × 9, you can use the diagram below to calculate 74 × 15, partitioning the 15 into 6 + 9.

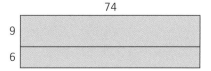

Q12.19: Now that you know 74 × 15, use the diagram below to calculate 74 × 39.

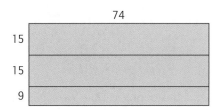

Q12.20: Use a diagram like this and results you already know to calculate 74 × 63.

Q12.21: Now do 74 × 63 by long multiplication and check that you get the same answer!

Questions 12.22–28: Learning and teaching (written methods for multiplication and division)

Questions 12.22–24 are about the teaching of multiplication calculations.

Q12.22: To introduce the areas method for multiplication, a teacher puts up a rectangular array of 12 squares by 15 squares to illustrate 12 × 15. How might the teacher proceed from here?

Q12.23: A parent complains about the grid method for multiplication, asking why the school cannot teach children the proper method of long multiplication. How might you respond to this?

Q12.24: Make a list of some key points to focus on in teaching for mastery of the long multiplication method for multiplying a two-digit number by a two-digit number. Use 47 × 36 as an example.

Questions 12.25–28 are about some common errors that children make in written multiplication and division calculations.

Q12.25: Identify and comment on the error in this calculation of 63 × 27.

$$
\begin{array}{r}
63 \\
\times \quad 27 \\
\hline
4221 \\
\underline{1260} \\
5481 \\
\end{array}
$$

Q12.26: Identify and comment on the error in this calculation of 20 × 10.

$$\begin{array}{r} 20 \\ \times \quad 10 \\ \hline 200 \\ 20 \\ \hline 220 \end{array}$$

Q12.27: Identify and comment on the error in this calculation of 52 × 24.

$$\begin{array}{r} 54 \\ \times \quad 24 \\ \hline \end{array}$$

$$\begin{array}{rcr} 2 \times 50 & = & 100 \\ 2 \times 2 & = & 4 \\ 4 \times 50 & = & 200 \\ 4 \times 2 & = & 8 \\ \hline & & 312 \end{array}$$

Q12.28: Identify and comment on the error in this calculation of 800 ÷ 25.

$$\begin{array}{r} 36 \\ 25\overline{)800} \\ 75 \\ \hline 150 \\ 150 \\ \hline 0 \end{array}$$

NATURAL NUMBERS: SOME KEY CONCEPTS

Questions related to Chapter 13 in *Mathematics Explained for Primary Teachers*, 7th edition.

Questions 13.01–24: Checking understanding (natural numbers: some key concepts)

For **Questions 13.01–03** use the concepts of 'is a factor of' and 'is a multiple of'.

Q13.01: Using an arrow from one number to another to represent 'is a factor of', draw all the possible arrows in the diagram below.

Q13.02: Now do the same as in Question 13.01, but using an arrow to represent 'is a multiple of'.

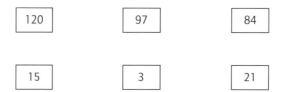

Q13.03: Write down some interesting observations arising from your responses to Questions 13.01 and 13.02.

For each of **Questions 13.04–13**, decide whether the statement is true or false.

Q13.04: 68 is a factor of 17.

Q13.05: 1 is a factor of every natural number.

Q13.06: If a is a multiple of b, then b must be a factor of a.

Q13.07: If you double a natural number then you double its digital sum.

Q13.08: The digital root of 123,456,789 is 9.

Q13.09: The number 123,456,789 is a multiple of 9.

Q13.10: If 12 is a factor of a number z, then z must be a multiple of 3.

Q13.11: The lowest common multiple of 6 and 12 is 24.

Q13.12: There are no prime numbers between 89 and 97.

Q13.13: There are no even prime numbers.

Questions 13.14–17 are an opportunity to be pedantic! Each of the given 'definitions' is either slightly wrong or imprecise in some respect. Rewrite them without any errors or lack of precision.

Q13.14: A multiple of 7 is a whole number that can be divided by 7.

Q13.15: A factor of 280 is a number that 280 can be divided by.

Q13.16: A prime number is a number that does not have any factors.

Q13.17: A rectangular or composite number is a number that can be represented by one or more rows of counters.

For **Questions 13.18–21** find a number lying between 120 and 140 that satisfies the given condition.

Q13.18: The number is a square number.

Q13.19: The number is a cube number.

Q13.20: The number is a triangle number.

Q13.21: The number is the product of three different prime numbers.

For each of **Questions 13.22–24**, insert the correct inequality sign (> or <) in the gap(s).

Q13.22: 10 … $\sqrt{50}$

Q13.23: $\sqrt[3]{100}$ … 5

Q13.24: 8 … $\sqrt{70}$ … 9

Questions 13.25-40: Reasoning and problem solving (natural numbers: some key concepts)

Questions 13.25–28 are about a famous unproven theorem, called Goldbach's conjecture (Christian Goldbach, 1690–1764).

Q13.25: Can you find two prime numbers that have a sum of 22?

Q13.26: Can you find two prime numbers that have a sum of 23?

Q13.27: Goldbach's conjecture is that every even number greater than 2 is the sum of two prime numbers. For example, 52 = 5 + 47. Test this conjecture with all the even numbers from 4 to 30.

Q13.28: Some odd numbers are also the sum of two primes. Which ones?

Questions 13.29–31 are an assortment of problems using multiples, factors and primes.

Q13.29: A flower grower supplies boxes of flowers to various flower sellers. Some like to sell the flowers in bunches of 5, others in bunches of 8 and others in bunches of 12. What is the smallest number of flowers that the flower grower should put in each box to satisfy all the flower sellers? What mathematical idea is being used here?

Q13.30: Find the smallest number that is a multiple of all the natural numbers from 1 to 10 inclusive.

Q13.31: Investigate the conjecture that 'there are at least two prime numbers in every decade'. Take the decades to be 1–10, 11–20, 21–30 and so on.

Questions 13.32–35 use rectangles drawn on a grid to explore one of the mathematical ideas in Chapter 13 of *Mathematics Explained*. A 'point on the grid' is a point where two grid lines intersect.

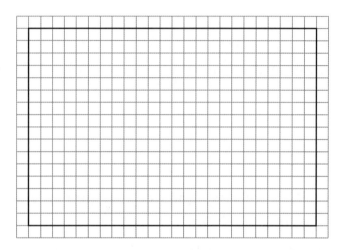

Q13.32: The diagram provided is a rectangle of 24 units by 16 units. Draw carefully with a ruler the diagonal from the bottom left-hand corner to the top right-hand corner. Not counting the starting point, through how many points on the grid does the diagonal pass?

Q13.33: How is your answer to Question 13.32 related to the numbers 24 and 16? (Look for one of the mathematical ideas explained in Chapter 13 of *Mathematics Explained*.)

Q13.34: Repeat this with other rectangles, such as one that is 15 units by 20 units. (Grids for your own drawings are provided at the end of this book.)

Q13.35: Summarize and explain what you discover.

Questions 13.36–40 are five investigations involving squares and cubes for you to try.

Q13.36: Is the sum of two square numbers a square number? Always, sometimes, never?

Q13.37: Is the product of two square numbers a square number? Always, sometimes, never?

Q13.38: Investigate the following sequence and find a relationship with the triangle numbers:

1^3

$1^3 + 2^3$

$1^3 + 2^3 + 3^3$

$1^3 + 2^3 + 3^3 + 4^3$

$1^3 + 2^3 + 3^3 + 4^3 + 5^3$

and so on.

Q13.39: Use a calculator. Choose a number. First, square it then cube the answer. Second, cube it and square the answer. Are the results the same? Is this always the case?

Q13.40: Is there a number between 1 and 100 that is both a cube number and a square number?

Questions 13.41–54: Learning and teaching (natural numbers: some key concepts)

Questions 13.41–42 are two classroom-based examples.

Q13.41: For a mathematics task, Jake, a ten-year-old, put out some counters as shown. Suggest some problems that Jake might have been investigating. Make at least three suggestions, using some of the key mathematical language and concepts in Chapter 13 of *Mathematics Explained*.

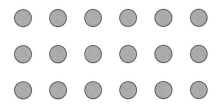

Q13.42: In a discussion about factors, an 11-year-old said: 'Factors always come in twos, don't they? Like, with 28, you get 1 and 28, 2 and 14, 4 and 7.' How would you, as a teacher, respond to this and turn it into a useful learning opportunity?

Questions 13.43–45 provide extracts from three lesson plans prepared by trainee teachers for introducing the concept of prime numbers to a group of children aged 10–11 years. What do you think of these ideas? Which seems to you to be the best approach and which the worst? Why?

Q13.43: This is Plan A for you to evaluate.

- Remind children of the meaning of 'factor', using the factors of 20 as an example (1, 2, 4, 5, 10, 20).
- Display the definition of a prime number.
- Use this to explain why 7 is a prime number but 8 is not.
- Work through these examples to check whether or not they are prime numbers: 10, 11, 12, 13 and 14.
- Then get the children to check 15, 16, 17, 18, 19 and 20.

Q13.44: This is Plan B for you to evaluate.

- Revise the concept of 'factor' by asking the children to give factors of 30. Make sure they include 1 and 30.
- Draw a large circle on the board and label it set P. Tell the children that in my head I have a rule, which is something to do with factors. If a number satisfies this rule, it goes into set P.
- Ask the children to suggest numbers from 2 to 50 and write them on the board, either inside or outside set P, depending on whether or not they are prime. Once there are three numbers in P, ask the children to suggest a number and to say whether or not they think it goes in set P.
- When some children are consistently identifying members of set P, ask the children in groups to discuss what they think might be my rule.
- Share ideas and, by questioning, lead the children to articulate the rule: 'The number has just two factors, 1 and itself.' Now tell the children that P stands for 'prime numbers'.
- Fill in the missing numbers from 2 to 50.

Q13.45: This is Plan C for you to evaluate.

- Say there are 28 children in the class. Ask them how they could be put into teams for a quiz, with the same number in each team. A team has to have more than one person in it.
- Get one of the children to put 28 children in the class into 7 teams of 4 as an example.
- Write up all the different arrangements: 2 teams of 14, 14 teams of 2, 4 teams of 7, 7 teams of 4. Show these with 28 counters arranged in rectangular arrays.

- Ask the children in groups to do the same for a class of 30 children.
- Then raise the question of putting a class of 29 children into teams.
- Discuss how 29 is different from 28 and 30. Use the word 'factor'. How many factors did we find for 28? For 30? But for 29, there are only two factors, 1 and 29, so we can't split 29 into teams of the same number.
- Ask the children in groups to find other numbers like this, using counters if they wish. Share results and introduce the term 'prime number'.

Questions 13.46–47 relate to an activity to use with primary school children. Put two numbers on the board (for example, 16 and 36) and ask the children to find as many things as they can that are the same about these two numbers. They should form sentences beginning with the words, 'They both …' or 'They are both …'.

Q13.46: For the two numbers 16 and 36, list some of the sentences that children might come up with, using as many different mathematical ideas as possible.

Q13.47: What would you see as being the particular value of this activity? What kind of thinking does it encourage?

Questions 13.48–49 relate to a sequence of number shapes, the first four of which are shown below.

Q13.48: What numbers are represented by this sequence of shapes?

Q13.49: How could you use this sequence with older primary school children to discover the following pattern: $1 + 3 = 2^2$, $1 + 3 + 5 = 3^2$, $1 + 3 + 5 + 7 = 4^2$ and so on?

The activity described in **Questions 13.50–53** is the kind of experience that helps older primary children to recognize the importance sometimes of being very systematic in mathematical problem solving.

Q13.50: On a school weekend camp, there are two activities available on Friday and Saturday evenings – football (F) or chess (C). Children can choose either activity each evening. This means that there are four possible options available to the children. Three of these are FF, FC and CC, where, for example, FC means football on the first evening and chess on the second. What is the fourth option?

Q13.51: How many options would be available if there were *three* activities to choose from each evening – football (F), chess (C) or music (M)?

Q13.52: How would you develop this idea and make a connection with square numbers?

Q13.53: How could it be developed further and connected with cube numbers?

Question 13.54 is about an error in the Year 5 Programme of Study for the Mathematics National Curriculum for England (2013), where we read that pupils should learn about 'composite (non-prime) numbers'.

Q13.54: What's wrong with suggesting that 'composite number' is synonymous with 'non-prime number'?

INTEGERS: POSITIVE AND NEGATIVE

Questions related to Chapter 14 in *Mathematics Explained for Primary Teachers*, 7th edition.

Questions 14.01–14.17: Checking understanding (integers: positive and negative)

For **Questions 14.01–14.03** insert the correct inequality sign (> or <) in the gap between the integers given.

Q14.01: $(-7) \ldots (-4)$

Q14.02: $(0) \ldots (-4)$

Q14.03: $(+16) \ldots (-20) \ldots (-99)$

Questions 14.04–14.07 are for practising addition involving negative integers.

Q14.04: If the temperature rises by 9 °C from −2 °C, what is the new temperature?

Q14.05: My bank account has a balance of −47 pounds. If I now pay in 25 pounds, what is the new balance?

Q14.06: Find the sum of −8 and +8.

Q14.07: Find the sum of −1, −3, −6 and +8.

Questions 14.08–14.12 are for practising the subtraction of integers in the context of temperature.

Q14.08: What is the difference between a temperature of +12 °C and one of −2 °C?

Q14.09: What is the difference between a temperature of −6 °C and one of −2 °C?

Q14.10: What is the difference between a temperature of −7 °C and one of +5 °C?

Q14.11: Show the calculations in Questions 14.08, 14.09 and 14.10 as comparisons on number line diagrams.

Q14.12: Write the calculations in Questions 14.08, 14.09 and 14.10 in the form $p − q = r$, where p, q and r are integers.

Questions 14.13–14.17 are for practising the subtraction of integers in the context of a bank balance.

Q14.13: What must be added to my bank account if the current balance is £17 in credit and I want to be £25 in credit?

Q14.14: What must be added to my bank account if the current balance is £5 overdrawn and I want to be £10 in credit?

Q14.15: What must be added to my bank account if the current balance is £12 overdrawn and I want to be only £5 overdrawn?

Q14.16: Show the calculations in Questions 14.13, 14.14 and 14.15 on number line diagrams using the idea of inverse of addition.

Q14.17: Write the calculations in Questions 14.13, 14.14 and 14.15 in the form $p − q = r$, where p, q and r are positive integers for credits and negative integers for overdrafts.

Questions 14.18–14.27: Reasoning and problem solving (integers: positive and negative)

Questions 14.18–14.20 refer to the following data:

The bottom of the Marianas Trench in the northern Pacific Ocean is about 10,920 metres below sea level.

The bottom of the Java Trench in the Indian Ocean is about 7130 metres below sea level.

The bottom of the Puerto Rico Trench in the Atlantic Ocean is about 8600 metres below sea level.

The summit of Mount Everest in the Himalayas is about 8850 metres above sea level.

The summit of Mount McKinley in Alaska is about 5500 metres above sea level.

The summit of Mount Kilimanjaro in Tanzania is about 5890 metres above sea level.

Q14.18:   Which of the bottom of the Java Trench and the bottom of the Puerto Rico Trench is nearer the surface of the sea and by how much? What calculation did you do to work this out?

Q14.19:   Make up a question about this data that corresponds to the subtraction 8850 – (–8600) and answer it.

Q14.20:   Make up some other questions you could ask about this data. Answer your own questions. What calculations with positive and negative integers correspond to your questions and answers?

For **Question 14.21** you need to know that a magic square is a square array of numbers in which the numbers in each of the rows, columns and the two main diagonals add up to the same total.

Q14.21:   In the grid below, fill in the missing numbers so that it becomes a magic square using all the integers from –12 to 12.

4	11	–12	–5	
		–6		3
	–7	0		9
		6	8	
–2		12		–4

Questions 14.22–14.27 provide a way of 'explaining' what happens when two negative numbers are multiplied together, based on the pattern in a multiplication table.

Q14.22:   On a number line, a negative integer could represent a movement of so many units in the negative direction. The diagram below shows how –4 could be interpreted as a movement of 4 units to the left. Use this idea to explain why a negative integer multiplied by a positive integer gives a negative answer. For example, (–4) × 3 = –12.

Q14.23:   Which principle of multiplication would then justify the result 3 × (–4) = –12?

Q14.24:   The multiplication table below already contains the products of pairs of integers from the set: 0, 1, 2, 3, 4, together with the results obtained in

Questions 14.22 and 14.23. Use the idea of repeated movements in a negative direction and the property referred to in Question 14.22 to fill in the shaded squares.

×	−4	−3	−2	−1	0	1	2	3	4
−4								−12	
−3									
−2									
−1									
0					0	0	0	0	0
1					0	1	2	3	4
2					0	2	4	6	8
3	−12				0	3	6	9	12
4					0	4	8	12	16

Q14.25: Notice the patterns in the sequences of numbers in the rows and columns in this table. Continue these patterns to fill in the remaining squares in the multiplication table.

Q14.26: What is shown here about multiplying together two negative numbers?

Q14.27: I am thinking of a number which when squared is equal to 16. What might my number be?

Questions 14.28–14.36: Learning and teaching (integers: positive and negative)

In **Questions 14.28–14.29** we consider how a simple number game involving moving counters along a number strip might be adapted to include negative numbers.

Q14.28: Many simple games use a number strip, as shown below. In this example, each player starts with their counter on zero and then in turn throws a conventional die with faces labelled 1 to 6. They move on the number of squares indicated by the die. Encourage the children to predict where they will land before they do the counting on. If they land on a shaded square, they have to go back 5 spaces. The first one to reach (or pass) 25 is the winner. Predict where a player's counter would be if their first three throws of the die are 2, 4 and 5.

0	1	2	3	4	5	6	7	8	9	10	11	12	13	14	15	16	17	18	19	20	21	22	23	24	25

Q14.29: How might you adapt this game so that it can be used to introduce younger children to negative integers in a meaningful context?

In **Questions 14.30–14.34** the calculations given are incorrect. Correct them and suggest how you might explain to an 11-year-old how these calculations might be understood.

Q14.30: $5 - 8 = 3$

Q14.31: $6 + (-8) = -14$

Q14.32: $5 - (-8) = -3$

Q14.33: $-5 - (-8) = -13$

Q14.34: $0 - 9 = 9$

Questions 14.35–14.36 are about responses from two nine-year-olds asked about the largest and smallest numbers in this set of integers: -99, 0, -42 and 45.

Q14.35: One child says that -99 is the largest number in the set. How would you respond to this?

Q14.36: Another child says that 0 is the smallest number in the set. How would you respond to this?

FRACTIONS AND RATIOS

Questions related to Chapter 15 in *Mathematics Explained for Primary Teachers*, 7th edition.

Questions 15.01–20: Checking understanding (fractions and ratios)

For **Questions 15.01–05** use the fraction chart showing the relationships between halves, fifths and tenths.

1									
½					½				
⅕		⅕		⅕		⅕		⅕	
¹⁄₁₀	¹⁄₁₀	¹⁄₁₀	¹⁄₁₀	¹⁄₁₀	¹⁄₁₀	¹⁄₁₀	¹⁄₁₀	¹⁄₁₀	¹⁄₁₀

Q15.01: List all the examples of equivalent fractions shown in the chart.

Q15.02: Find a fraction equivalent to $\frac{1}{2} + \frac{1}{10}$.

Q15.03: Add $\frac{1}{5}$ and $\frac{3}{10}$.

Q15.04: Find a fraction equivalent to $\frac{7}{10} - \frac{1}{5}$.

Q15.05: Find the difference between $\frac{4}{5}$ and $\frac{1}{2}$.

Questions 15.06–11 are assorted questions about fractions and ratios in different contexts.

Q15.06: For each of the figures P, Q and R, state what fraction of the shape is shaded.

  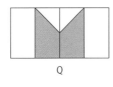 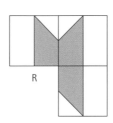

P   Q   R

Q15.07: Three-eighths of a class of 32 children are 8 years of age. How many are not 8 years of age?

Q15.08: An area of three square metres of a flower bed, as shown below, is shared equally between 8 children. What fraction of a square metre does each get?

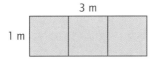

3 m

1 m

Q15.09: Two children, Amy and Ben, have £88 between them. Amy has £33. What fraction of the £88 does Amy have? What is the ratio of Amy's share to Ben's share, in its simplest form?

Q15.10: What point on the number line comes halfway between 0 and $^3/_4$?

Q15.11: Consider the inequality statement, $^1/_2 <$ ☐ $< ^2/_3$. Write a fraction in the box that makes the statement correct.

In **Questions 15.12–20** decide whether the given statement is true or false.

Q15.12: $^7/_{12}$ of £36 is £21.

Q15.13: $^5/_6 < ^4/_5$.

Q15.14: In the fraction $^7/_{10}$ the 10 is the numerator.

Q15.15: A top-heavy fraction like $^{17}/_{10}$ is also called an imperfect fraction.

Q15.16: $^{75}/_{90}$ and $^5/_6$ are equivalent fractions.

Q15.17: If two salaries are in the ratio 5:6, then one is $^5/_6$ of the other.

Q15.18: 25:500 and 2:40 are equivalent ratios.

Q15.19: If there are 4 daffodils in a bunch of 12 flowers, then the ratio of daffodils to other flowers is 1:3.

Q15.20: $^7/_{10}$ is less than three-quarters.

Questions 15.21-30: Reasoning and problem solving (fractions and ratios)

Questions 15.21–24 are four examples of fractions used in real-life contexts.

Q15.21: Assuming all the books are the same price, which is the better buy: three books for the price of two? Or, buy one get a second book half price?

Q15.22: A confusing advertisement at my local garden centre said: 'Sale: up to half price!' Do you think that what this actually said was what the garden centre intended?

Q15.23: This question illustrates a common example of lack of clarity in using fractions. A year ago there were 200 children in a school, of which 80 were having school lunches every day. This year the headteacher reports:

'The proportion of children having school lunches every day has increased by a fifth since last year.' Why is this ambiguous? If there are still 200 children in the school, what two different things might the statement mean?

Q15.24: A school has 275 children on the school roll. Next year this increases by a fifth. Then the following year it decreases by a fifth. What is the number of children on the school roll at this point?

Questions 15.25–27 reveal a pattern in adding fractions that have 1 as the numerator.

Q15.25: (a) What is the sum of 3 and 4? (b) What is the product of 3 and 4? (c) What is the sum of $\frac{1}{3}$ and $\frac{1}{4}$? (d) How does the answer to (c) relate to the answers to (a) and (b)?

Q15.26: Repeat question 15.25, using the two numbers 5 and 8. Relate their sum and product to the sum of $\frac{1}{5}$ and $\frac{1}{8}$?

Q15.27: Try this again with two numbers of your choice and formulate in words a generalization.

Questions 15.28–30 are problem-solving tasks using fractions.

Q15.28: Using only positive integers, find all the possibilities for the two missing numbers in these equivalent fractions. You do not have to put the same number in each box.

$$\frac{12}{\Box} = \frac{\Box}{12}$$

Q15.29: A strip of ribbon of length 280 cm is cut so that one piece is three-quarters of the length of the other. What are the lengths of the two pieces?

Q15.30: This problem has a unique solution. In a school with fewer than 500 children, exactly $\frac{2}{7}$ of the children have school lunches, exactly $\frac{3}{10}$ walk to school, exactly $\frac{3}{4}$ live within 2 miles of the school, and exactly $\frac{2}{3}$ have a 100% attendance record one term. How many children are in the school? How many are in each of these categories?

Questions 15.31–42: Learning and teaching (fractions and ratios)

Questions 15.31–35 challenge you to make up questions for children aged 9–11 years that use the five different interpretations of a fraction (in this case, $\frac{2}{3}$) identified in Chapter 15 of *Mathematics Explained*.

Q15.31: Make up a question related to a geometric shape that interprets the fraction $^2/_3$ as a proportion of a unit.

Q15.32: Make up a question that interprets the fraction $^2/_3$ as a point on a number line.

Q15.33: Make up a question related to the number of children in the class that interprets the fraction $^2/_3$ as a proportion of a set.

Q15.34: Make up a question about three children sharing that interprets the fraction $^2/_3$ as the division of 2 by 3.

Q15.35: Make up a question where two numbers or quantities are compared that interprets the fraction $^2/_3$ as a ratio.

Questions 15.36–37 are examples of children's errors with fractions.

Q15.36: How would you respond to a child who draws these diagrams and concludes that $^4/_6$ and $^3/_4$ are equal?

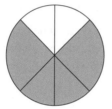 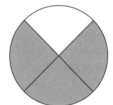

Q15.37: An 11-year-old states that a half added to a third is a fifth. How would you help this child to correct the misunderstanding here?

Questions 15.38–40 are three teaching plans for helping children understand why $^1/_2 > ^1/_3 > ^1/_4 > ^1/_5 > ^1/_6$ and so on. Comment on each plan and decide which plan you would prefer and why.

Q15.38: This is Plan A for you to evaluate.

- Start by comparing $^1/_2$ with $^1/_3$.
- Explain to the children how to change $^1/_2$ to sixths by multiplying the top and bottom by 3.
- Then ask the children to change $^1/_2$ to sixths by multiplying the top and bottom by 2.
- Ask the children which is the greater, $^3/_6$ or $^2/_6$?
- Then look at $^1/_3$ and $^1/_4$. Ask what kinds of fractions we could change them both into (twelfths). Follow the same procedure as before.
- Record on the board as each comparison is made: $^1/_2 > ^1/_3$, $^1/_3 > ^1/_4$ and so on.

Q15.39: This is Plan B for you to evaluate.

- Take the class into the hall. Count out a group of 24 children. Ask these children to sort themselves into two equal groups. What fraction is each group of the set of 24? Answer: a half.
- Now ask them to sort themselves into three equal groups. What fraction is each group now of the 24? (Answer: a third.) Are there more or fewer children in each group than when there were only two groups?
- Then into four equal groups. Then six. Then eight.
- Through question, answer and discussion, establish that the more groups there are the smaller the groups.
- Make a connection with the bottom number in the fraction, which tells us how many groups.

Q15.40: This is Plan C for you to evaluate.

- On the board, draw a series of equal rectangles, which represent chocolate bars. Divide the first one into halves, the second into thirds, the next into quarters, the next into fifths and so on.
- Ask the children who would get the most chocolate: someone having $\frac{1}{2}$ of a bar, someone having $\frac{1}{3}$ of a bar, someone having $\frac{1}{4}$ of a bar and so on, comparing the fractions in the diagram.
- Record on the board as each comparison is made: $\frac{1}{2} > \frac{1}{3} > \frac{1}{4} > \frac{1}{5} > \frac{1}{6}$ and so on.

Questions 15.41–42 relate to this assessment item for children around 10 to 11 years:

- To divide the given rectangle into 3 equal parts (thirds), you need to draw 2 lines.
- To divide it into 5 equal parts (fifths), you need to draw 4 lines.
- How many lines do you need to draw to divide the rectangle into 7 equal parts (sevenths)?
- 9 equal parts (ninths)?
- 4 equal parts (quarters)?

Q15.41: Answer these questions yourself.

Q15.42: What do you think is the main point of this task in terms of assessing children's mathematical ability?

DECIMAL NUMBERS AND ROUNDING

Questions related to Chapter 16 in *Mathematics Explained for Primary Teachers*, 7th edition.

Questions 16.01–24: Checking understanding (decimal numbers and rounding)

For **Questions 16.01–02** put the given numbers in order, from smallest to largest.

Q16.01:   75.09, 75.9, 57.9, 59.07, 57.09, 79.5, 79.05

Q16.02:   0.00345, 0.03054, 0.04, 0.00543, 0.053, 0.3, 0.0035

Questions 16.03–07 are about connecting decimal numbers to various images and materials.

Q16.03:   Draw arrows to show approximately where on this number line would be the numbers 0.209 and 0.290.

Q16.04:   Approximately, what are the numbers indicated by the arrows on this number line?

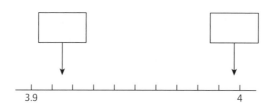

Q16.05:   See the picture of base-ten Dienes blocks in Question 6.16. Assume that a flat is taken to represent a unit. What number is represented by 3 large cubes, 4 flats and 3 longs?

Q16.06:   Megan finds that the length of her classroom is the same as 5 metre rods, 29 decimetre rods and 16 centimetre cubes. How long is this in centimetres?

Q16.07:   See Q16.06 above. How long is the classroom in metres?

For **Questions 16.08–11** use a calculator to find $379 \div 49$.

Q16.08: Round the calculator answer to the nearest whole number.

Q16.09: Round the answer to one decimal place.

Q16.10: Round the answer to three significant digits.

Q16.11: Round the answer to four decimal places.

Questions 16.12–18 are about interpreting the result of the division $263 \div 15$. First, do this division on a calculator and write down the result displayed.

Q16.12: How many teams of 15 can be formed from 263 children? (Use the calculator result.)

Q16.13: What do the figures after the decimal point in the calculator answer represent in Question 16.12?

Q16.14: How much does each child get when 263p is shared between 15 children? (Use the calculator result.)

Q16.15: What do the figures after the decimal point in the calculator answer represent in Question 16.14?

Q16.16: Do the division by a non-calculator method to obtain an answer with a remainder.

Q16.17: What does the remainder in Question 16.16 represent if the division was being done to answer Question 16.12?

Q16.18: What does the remainder in Question 16.16 represent if the division was being done to answer Question 16.14?

In **Questions 16.19–24** decide whether the statements are correct or incorrect equivalences between fractions and decimals numbers.

Q16.19: $0.125 = \frac{1}{8}$

Q16.20: $\frac{7}{8} = 0.825$

Q16.21: $\frac{23}{10} = 0.23$

Q16.22: $0.034 = \frac{34}{1000}$

Q16.23: $\frac{2}{9} = 0.2222\ldots$ (with the 2 recurring)

Q16.24: $\frac{3}{5} = 0.15$

Questions 16.25–42: Reasoning and problem solving (decimal numbers and rounding)

For **Questions 16.25–28** you are told that I need to save £3000.

Q16.25:   If I set up a standing order to save £132 a month, how many months will it take me to reach my target? Enter one calculation on a calculator to model this problem and deduce the real-world solution.

Q16.26:   If I set up a standing order of £96 a month, how many months will it take me to reach my target? Enter one calculation on a calculator to model this problem and deduce the real-world solution.

Q16.27:   For each of the calculator results in Questions 16.25 and 16.26, decide whether it is: (a) an exact, appropriate answer; (b) an exact but inappropriate answer; or (c) an answer that has been truncated?

Q16.28:   Did the calculator answers in Questions 16.25 and 16.26 have to be rounded up or rounded down in obtaining the real-world solution?

Questions 16.29–32: Jo knows that there are 365 days in a (non-leap) year and 7 days in a week. She wants to work out how many weeks there are in a year.

Q16.29:   What is the mathematical model of Jo's problem?

Q16.30:   Use a non-calculator method to solve the mathematical problem, giving the answer with a remainder. What is the answer to Jo's question? What is the meaning of the remainder?

Q16.31:   Now obtain the mathematical solution using a calculator. Is this calculator answer: an exact, appropriate answer; an exact but inappropriate answer; or an answer that has been truncated?

Q16.32:   What do the figures after the decimal point in the calculator answer represent?

To answer **Questions 16.33–36**, decide what calculation you need to enter on a calculator, do this on a calculator and then interpret the answer.

Q16.33:   What is the cost of 0.780 kg of cheddar cheese priced at £3.45 per kilogram?

Q16.34:   How much cheddar cheese priced at £3.45 per kilogram could you buy with £15?

Q16.35:   How many times larger than a school playground of area 3640 square metres is a football pitch of area 8450 square metres?

Q16.36:   How many buses, each holding 56 passengers, are required to transport a school party of 325 individuals?

Questions 16.37–38 refer to the table below, showing some historic data for TV audience figures for the most watched television show in the UK in various years from 1984 to 2020.

1986	*Eastenders* (25 December)	30.1 million
1987	*Eastenders* (1 January)	28 million
1996	*Only Fools and Horses* (28 December)	24.35 million
1997	Funeral of Princess Diana (6 September)	19.29 million
1998	World Cup, England v. Argentina (30 June)	23.78 million
2007	*Eastenders* (25 December)	14.38 million
2008	*Eastenders* (25 December)	16.15 million
2016	*The Great British Bake Off* (26 October)	15.9 million
2017	*Blue Planet II* (29 October)	14.01 million

Q16.37: What is wrong with the way the data has been presented in this table? It will help you to think about the rounding that must have been applied to the raw data here.

Q16.38: If another programme, not listed, had viewing figures of 27.64 million, would that be smaller than the audience for *Eastenders* on 1 January 1987?

Questions 16.39–42 reveal a fascinating property of sevenths expressed as recurring decimals.

Q16.39: Using short division, divide 1 by 7 and find a recurring decimal equivalent to the fraction $^1/_7$ (with six digits recurring).

Q16.40: Double the result in Question 16.39 and hence find a recurring decimal equivalent to $^2/_7$.

Q16.41: Add the results in Questions 16.39 and 16.40 and hence find a recurring decimal equivalent to $^3/_7$.

Q16.42: Look carefully at the recurring decimal equivalents of $^1/_7$, $^2/_7$ and $^3/_7$. Can you spot something interesting about these? If so, predict the recurring decimal equivalents for $^4/_7$, $^5/_7$ and $^6/_7$.

Questions 16.43-50: Learning and teaching (decimal numbers and rounding)

For **Questions 16.43–46** analyse the misunderstandings shown and suggest ways of helping the child.

Q16.43: An eight-year-old calculates the cost of 6 items at £1.65 each on a calculator, gets the result 9.9 and says that the total cost is 'nine pounds nine pence'.

Q16.44: A nine-year-old reads 3.45 as 'three point forty-five'.

Q16.45: A boy aged 11 years measures the length and width of a rectangular classroom as 7 metres and 5 metres, to the nearest metre. By adding two lengths and two widths, he works out that the perimeter is 24 metres to the nearest metre. What questions might a teacher ask to encourage him to reconsider his conclusion?

Q16.46: A girl aged 11 years is continuing a sequence counting in tenths and writes down '3.4, 3.5, 3.6, 3.7, 3.8, 3.9, 3.10 …'.

For **Questions 16.47–48** assume that you are aiming to introduce some children to the idea that answers are rounded up or down depending on the context.

Q16.47: Make up two questions, to use in a class discussion, involving 28 ÷ 6, using the context of a class of 28 children, one where the answer is 4 and the other where the answer is 5.

Q16.48: Now do this again using the same numbers as in Question 16.47 but in the context of money.

For **Questions 16.49–50** consider an 11-year-old who is calculating 250 ÷ 35. She knows about equivalent ratios, so she decides to simplify the calculation by dividing both numbers by 5, to get 50 ÷ 7. This gives her the solution 7 remainder 1. She also does the calculation 50 ÷ 7 on a calculator and gets the answer 7.1428571.

Q16.49: Which one of these is the correct answer to the original question, 250 ÷ 35?

Q16.50: How would you help her to see that the other one is incorrect?

CALCULATIONS WITH DECIMALS

Questions related to Chapter 17 in *Mathematics Explained for Primary Teachers*, 7th edition.

Questions 17.01-19: Checking understanding (calculations with decimals)

Questions 17.01–02 are about changing units of measurement to simplify calculations with decimals.

Q17.01: 'If my stride is 0.85 m, how far do I walk in 24 paces?' Recast this question in centimetres to remove the decimal point, do the calculation (without a calculator) and interpret the answer as a distance in metres.

Q17.02: 'How many glasses of 0.15 litres can be poured from a 2.5-litre bottle of water?' Recast this question in centilitres (100 centilitres = 1 litre) to remove the decimal points, do the calculation (without a calculator) and answer the question.

Questions 17.03–06 are about repeatedly multiplying and dividing decimal numbers by 10.

Q17.03: $0.03985 \times 10 \times 10 = ?$

Q17.04: $0.03985 \times 10 \times 10 \times 10 \times 10 \times 10 \times 10 = ?$

Q17.05: $4683 \div 10 \div 10 \div 10 = ?$

Q17.06: $4683 \div 10 \div 10 \div 10 \div 10 \div 10 \div 10 = ?$

For **Questions 17.07–16** determine whether the result is correct or incorrect. (No calculator allowed!)

Q17.07: $100 - 65.43 = 35.57$

Q17.08: $5 \times 0.42 = 2.1$

Q17.09: $(0.095 \times 2) > 0.32$

Q17.10: $9.06 \div 3 = 3.2$

Q17.11: $10 \div 0.5 = 2$

Q17.12: $2.40 \times 3.01 = 0.7224$

Q17.13: $0.2 \times 0.2 = 0.4$

Q17.14: $25 \text{ million} = 2.5 \times 10 \times 10 \times 10 \times 10 \times 10 \times 10$

Q17.15: $8 \div 10 \div 10 \div 10 > 7 \div 10 \div 10$

Q17.16: $(0.01)^2 = 0.0001$

Questions 17.17–19 are about the result of the division $320 \div 17$.

Q17.17: Use a non-calculator method to find the answer to this division in the form of a whole number with a remainder.

Q17.18: Use long division to calculate $320 \div 17$ to four decimal places. (Put the calculator away!)

Q17.19:   What is the relationship between the part after the decimal point in your answer to Question 17.18, the remainder in Question 17.17 and the divisor 17?

Questions 17.20–25: Reasoning and problem solving (calculations with decimals)

For **Questions 17.20–21** remember that there are 1000 millilitres in a litre and 1000 grams in a kilogram.

Q17.20:   Suggest a question in a real-life situation, in the context of liquid volume and capacity, that would be modelled by '1.500 – 0.125'. Answer your question without using a calculator.

Q17.21:   Suggest a question in a real-life situation, in the context of weighing, which would be modeled by '2.500 + 1.120'. Answer your question without using a calculator.

Questions 17.22–25 are four challenging mathematical puzzles using decimals.

Q17.22:   Fill in the missing numbers (*A*, *B*, *C*, *D*, *E*) in the grid below, so that the three numbers in each row, column and diagonal add up to the same total. Here's a hint to get you started: 8.66 + 0.12 + *A* must equal *E* + 7.44 + *A*.

8.66	0.12	*A*
B	5	7.44
C	*D*	*E*

Q17.23:   Find the digits represented by M and N in the following calculation: 3.M5 × M.4 = 1.NN

   [Hint: 1.NN is smaller than 3.M5]

Q17.24:   Find the digits represented by P and Q in the following calculation: 6.P7 ÷ 3Q = Q.PQ9

   [Hint: Q is easy to identify]

Q17.25:   How many 0.9s would you have to multiply together to get an answer less than 0.1? For example, 0.9 × 0.9 × 0.9 = 0.729, so it's more than 3. First make a guess, then try it out on a calculator.

Questions 17.26–36: Learning and teaching (calculations with decimals)

Questions 17.26–29 provide examples of children's errors in calculations with decimals. What are the likely causes of the errors? How would you help the children concerned?

Q17.26: $7.65 + 3.2 = 7.97$

Q17.27: $8 - 3.4 = 5.6$

Q17.28: $3.26 \times 0.5 = 0.163$

Q17.29: $8 \div 0.4 = 0.2$

Questions 17.30–32 refer specifically to the requirements of the English National Curriculum (2013) for Year 6 children (10–11 years). For the given objective, write three examples of context-free calculations that these children should be able to do. Answer your own questions and check with a calculator that you got them right!

Q17.30: Year 6 children are expected to be able to 'multiply and divide numbers by 10, 100 and 1000, giving answers up to three decimal places'.

Q17.31: Year 6 children are expected to be able to 'multiply one-digit numbers with up to two decimal places by whole numbers'.

Q17.32: Year 6 children are expected to be able to 'use written division methods in cases where the answer has up to two decimal places'. For this objective, assume that it refers to division by a whole number.

For **Questions 17.33–36** you are asked to consider how children might understand key ideas about calculations with decimals by making connections with pictures of rectangles.

Q17.33: How could you use a rectangle, 8 cm by 5 cm, to demonstrate the relationship between 5×8 and 5×0.8?

Q17.34: How could you use the same rectangle to demonstrate the relationship between 5×8 and 0.5×0.8?

Q17.35: How might you use the areas method for multiplication to explain 3×0.42, by partitioning the 0.42 into $0.40 + 0.02$?

Q17.36: How might you use the areas method for multiplication to explain 36×0.42, by partitioning the 36 into $30 + 6$ and the 0.42 into $0.40 + 0.02$?

PROPORTIONALITY AND PERCENTAGES

Questions related to Chapter 18 in *Mathematics Explained for Primary Teachers*, 7th edition.

Questions 18.01–15: Checking understanding (proportionality and percentages)

Use **Questions 18.01–04** to check your mastery of the use of direct proportion in the context of adapting recipes. Use informal, intuitive approaches as far as possible.

Q18.01:   A recipe for 4 cakes requires 50 grams of peanuts. Adapt it for 12 cakes.

Q18.02:   A recipe for 4 cakes requires 50 grams of peanuts. Adapt it for 10 cakes.

Q18.03:   A recipe for 10 cakes requires 125 grams of cocoa. Adapt it for 4 cakes.

Q18.04:   A recipe for 6 cakes requires 220 grams of flour. Adapt it for 11 cakes.

Questions 18.05–08 are related to a village of 1200 people, of whom 528 are over 50 years of age. Insert the missing numbers.

Q18.05:   528 out of 1200 is the same proportion as 264 out of □.

Q18.06:   264 out of □ is the same proportion as □ out of 300.

Q18.07:   □ out of 300 is the same proportion as □ out of 100.

Q18.08:   So the proportion of over-50s in the village is □ %.

In Questions 18.09–15 check your facility in converting between fractions, decimals and percentages.

Q18.09:   What fraction is equivalent to 0.75 and to 75%?

Q18.10:   Write 37% as a decimal and as a fraction.

Q18.11:   Write $^3/_{20}$ as a decimal and as a percentage.

Q18.12:   Write 0.16 as a percentage and as a fraction (in its simplest form).

Q18.13:   Write 1% as a decimal and as a fraction.

Q18.14:   Write $^6/_{25}$ as a decimal and as a percentage.

Q18.15:   Write 0.1% as a decimal and as a fraction.

Questions 18.16–23: Reasoning and problem solving (proportionality and percentages)

Answer **Question 18.16–17** intuitively first, and then do the maths.

Q18.16: A shop is advertising a computer for £600. The manager tells you that there must be 20% tax added to this price. However, he is also offering a 10% discount. Which would you prefer the manager to apply first? The tax or the discount?

Q18.17: I had £5000 in shares in a company, but yesterday the value of the shares went down by 20%. Then today there was a surprising 20% increase in the value of the shares? So, now what are my shares worth?

Questions 18.18–19 refer to a government scheme for gift aid, which allows charities to reclaim the income tax already paid by the person making a gift on the amount of their contribution. This is a good example of where facility with percentages is required if you really want to know what's happening to your money! For example, if I earn £100 and 20% tax is deducted from this, my net earnings are £80. If I give this £80 to a charity, they can reclaim the £20 tax from the government, so the gross gift is the £100 I earned before tax.

Q18.18: Rob wants to make a gross annual contribution of £2400 to a charity, taking advantage of the gift aid scheme whereby the charity recovers the 20% tax he has already paid. How much should he give a month?

Q18.19: Jan makes a gift-aided contribution of £450 a month to a charity. From this amount, 20% tax has already been deducted and can be reclaimed by the charity. How much is Jan's annual contribution to the charity actually worth?

Questions 18.20–23 are four examples of percentages being used to make ambiguous statements or claims in everyday life. Why are the statements here ambiguous?

Q18.20: In a well-known store, an item already reduced by 20% and then marked with a blue cross has 'a further 10% off'.

Q18.21: A political party spokesman announced that his party's share of the vote had gone up by 10% since the previous election.

Q18.22: A newspaper reports that the risk of dying in hospital after an operation *soars* towards the end of the week, claiming that the likelihood of dying after surgery on a Friday compared to a Monday increases by 49%. (For reference, the proportion of Monday patients who die after surgery is 0.55%.)

Q18.23:   A headline for a report on the results of national tests in a prestigious newspaper read: 50% of primary children fail to master English and maths. (You can assume that mastery of a subject for primary children meant achieving a particular level in the national tests at the end of Key Stage 2.)

Questions 18.24-33: Learning and teaching (proportionality and percentages)

Questions 18.24–26 are three errors or misunderstandings made by children. Analyse these and suggest how to respond to them.

Q18.24:   5% of £40 is £8.

Q18.25:   An item costing £60 is reduced by 20%, so now it costs £40.

Q18.26:   The price of an article goes up from £40 to £50. That's a 20% increase.

Questions 18.27–28 are two suggestions for how to teach someone how to find 35% of £40. Evaluate them.

Q18.27:   Ask them what 35% means (answer, $^{35}/_{100}$). Ask them to simplify this fraction (divide top and bottom by 5, to get $^{7}/_{20}$). So, we need to find $^{7}/_{20}$ of £40. Ask what $^{1}/_{20}$ of £40 is (answer, £2). So, what is $^{7}/_{20}$? (£14).

Q18.28:   Ask them what 10% of £40 is (answer, £4). So, if we know 10%, how can we find 20%? 5%? How can we use the results for 10%, 20% and 5% to work out 35%?

Questions 18.29–33 are some statements about percentages taken from newspapers, magazines and websites. How could you use material like this with older primary children to develop an understanding of percentages and how they are used?

Q18.29:   Sale! Up to 50% off womenswear and menswear!

Q18.30:   Today's survey: 'Do you expect tax rises after the general election?' Results: yes, 91%; no, 9%.

Q18.31:   Car insurance: 75% no claims bonus.

Q18.32:   Basic rate of income tax cut from 25% to 20%.

Q18.33:   Job vacancy for salesperson: 20% commission on all sales.

ALGEBRAIC REASONING

Questions related to Chapter 19 in *Mathematics Explained for Primary Teachers*, 7th edition.

Questions 19.01–27: Checking understanding (algebraic reasoning)

Questions 19.01–07 relate to a game in which I choose a positive whole number less than 50 and you have to reply immediately with the number that has to be added to twice my number to give a total of 100. In questions 19.03–07, fill in the gaps to check your understanding of some key algebraic terminology.

Q19.01:   If I choose 27 as the input, what is the outpout?

Q19.02:   The input set is {1, 2, 3, 4, … 50}. What is the output set?

Q19.03:   With an input set, a rule and an output set, this is an example of a ………

Q19.04:   My number is the ……… variable.

Q19.05:   Your number is the ……… variable.

Q19.06:   If my number is x and your number is y, then a …… for calculating your number is $y = 100 - 2x$.

Q19.07:   The variable y is a …… of x.

For **Questions 19.08–11** you are told that books in a particular series can be bought online for £6 each, plus a flat rate fee of £5 for postage and packing, regardless of how many are purchased.

Q19.08:   How much do you pay for 3 books? For 20 books?

Q19.09:   Now make a generalization: how much for n books?

Q19.10:   Answer this by mental calculation: how many books do you buy if the total cost is £53?

Q19.11: What equation have you solved in Question 19.10?

For **Questions 19.12–15** you are told that in a toy shop a teacher buys x xylophones and y yo-yos. The xylophones cost £8 each and the yo-yos cost £3 each.

Q19.12: What is the meaning of $x + y$?

Q19.13: What is the meaning of $3y$?

Q19.14: What is the meaning of $8x + 3y$?

Q19.15: Why was the choice of x and y for the variables in these question a bad choice?

In **Questions 19.16–18** explain the different ways the letter m is used in each statement.

Q19.16: The length of the car is 4 m.

Q19.17: Each car has 4 wheels; if there are m cars they will have $4m$ wheels in total.

Q19.18: Jack is in Class 4m.

Questions 19.19–23 are about a number n on a number line, as shown. The arrow points in the positive direction.

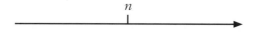

Q19.19: What is the number on the number line 5 units to the left of n? Check that your answer works when $n = -3$ and when $n = 3$.

Q19.20: Will $5n$ be to the left or the right of n?

Q19.21: What is the number midway between n and 20? Check that your answer works when $n = 50$ and when $n = -10$.

Q19.22: Give two numbers that are $2n$ units away from n?

Q19.23: If q is a number to the left of n and p is a number to the right of n, use inequality signs to connect the three variables, p, q and n.

For **Questions 19.24–27** you are told that p and q are positive, single-digit numbers.

Q19.24: $10p + q$ must be a two-digit number. True or false?

Q19.25: Find the two possible solutions to the equation $p + 5q = 19$.

Q19.26: Find the two possible solutions to the equation $3p - 4q = 1$.

Q19.27: Solve $8p = 9q$.

Questions 19.28–38: Reasoning and problem solving (algebraic reasoning)

Questions 19.28–30 refer to a booklet comprising several folded sheets of paper with 4 pages on each sheet. If the booklet were made from 5 folded sheets of paper, for example, it would have 20 pages. The centre pages would be numbered 10 and 11.

Q19.28: What page numbers would the centre pages be in a booklet made from just 1 sheet of paper? From 2 sheets? From 3 sheets? From 4 sheets?

Q19.29: What page numbers would the centre pages be in a booklet made from 50 sheets?

Q19.30: What would they be in a booklet made from n sheets?

Questions 19.31–34 explore some generalizations about points lying between two given points on a number line.

Q19.31: Assume that a and b are two points on a number line, with a less than b. The formula for the point x halfway between a and b is $x = \frac{1}{2}(a + b)$. Check this formula by trying $a = 10$ and $b = 70$.

Q19.32: The point y is a third of the way along from a to b. What would be the value of y if $a = 10$ and $b = 70$? Try some other values for a and b and try to come up with a formula for y.

Q19.33: The point z is a quarter of the way along from a to b. What would be the value of z if $a = 10$ and $b = 70$? Try some other values for a and b and try to come up with a formula for z.

Q19.34: Find a formula for the point p which is a sixth of the way along from a to b.

In **Questions 19.35–38** I think of a number (not necessarily a whole number), multiply it by 5, add 8 and then multiply by the number I thought of.

Q19.35: What is the result if the number I thought of was 6?

Q19.36: If the result is 580, what was the number I thought of?

Q19.37: If the result is 85, what was the number I thought of? You may need to use a calculator and trial and improvement.

Q19.38: If the number I think of is represented by x, what equation have you solved in Question 19.37?

Questions 19.39-51: Learning and teaching (algebraic reasoning)

For the activity in **Questions 19.39–41**, children are given the table below, asked to complete the bottom row and then to discuss the patterns in the numbers.

A	1	2	3	4	5	6	7	8	9	10	
B	4	7	10	13	16						

Q19.39:   What responses would you look for from children of various abilities?

Q19.40:   You then ask them what would be the value of the number in row B that would correspond to 100 in row A, writing 100 in the final box in the top row. What responses might you expect now?

Q19.41:   What would you make of a child entering 34 in the box below this?

Questions 19.42–43 relate to an algebra activity provided by a teacher of younger primary children. She has a pile of single-digit cards and announces that she is the 'add three person'. Whatever card she turns over, she adds three to the number shown. She turns over a card, looks at it and says, for example, 'seven'. The children have to work out the number on the card.

Q19.42:   In what way does this activity involve algebraic thinking? In what ways does it involve an independent variable and a dependent variable?

Q19.43:   How might the teacher develop this activity?

Questions 19.44–49 relate to a task for the assessment of Year 6 children's understanding of algebraic variables. The children are told that John and Sarah each have some money, and together they have £85. For this question we will say that John has x pounds and Sarah has y pounds.

Q19.44:   Decide when the statement '$x > 0$ and $y > 0$' is true. Always, sometimes or never?

Q19.45:   Decide when the statement '$x + y = 50$' is true. Always, sometimes or never?

Q19.46:   Decide when the statement '$x > y$' is true. Always, sometimes or never?

Q19.47:   Construct three similar assessment questions where the statement is always true.

Q19.48:   Construct three similar assessment questions where the statement is sometimes true (but not always).

Q19.49:   Construct three similar assessment questions where the statement is never true.

In **Questions 19.50–51** an 11-year-old is solving the equation $18 + 4x = 66$ by trying various values for x, and decides that the solution is $x = 3$.

Q19.50:   What should the solution be?

Q19.51:   What might have been the reason for the error and how would you respond to it?

COORDINATES AND LINEAR RELATIONSHIPS

Questions related to Chapter 20 in *Mathematics Explained for Primary Teachers*, 7th edition.

Questions 20.01–20: Checking understanding (coordinates and linear relationships)

For each of **Questions 20.01–07**, decide whether the statement is true or false.

Q20.01:   The straight-line graph representing a directly proportional relationship must always pass through $(0, 0)$.

Q20.02: $b = 3a + 2$ is a linear relationship between b and a.

Q20.03:   If $b = 3a + 2$, then b is directly proportional to a.

Q20.04:   If y is directly proportional to x, then when x is doubled, y is doubled.

Q20.05:   If y is directly proportional to x, then when x increases by 5, y must increase by 5.

Q20.06:   If the point $(15, 12)$ lies on a graph representing a linear relationship, then the point $(5, 4)$ must also lie on the graph.

Q20.07:   If the point $(15, 12)$ lies on a graph representing a directly proportional relationship, then the point $(5, 4)$ must also lie on the graph.

For each of **Questions 20.08–16** would you expect the variable y to be directly proportional to the variable x or not?

Q20.08: x grams is the mass (weight) of a package and £y is the cost of posting it.

Q20.09: x grams is the mass (weight) of cheese purchased and £y is the price paid.

Q20.10:   A sum of £x is exchanged for y Indian rupees (no additional charges).

Q20.11: x is the number of children in a primary school in a particular local authority and y is the number of teachers.

Q20.12: x miles per hour is the speed of a car and y metres is the stopping distance for an average driver.

Q20.13: A ball is thrown vertically upwards; x seconds is the time since the ball left the hand and y metres is the height of the ball from the ground.

Q20.14: x centimetres is the length of a side of a square and y centimetres is the perimeter of the square.

Q20.15: x centimetres is the length of a side of a square and y square centimetres is the area of the square.

Q20.16: A plumber charges £1 for each minute that a job takes, plus a £20 call-out charge. £y is the total charge for a job that takes x minutes.

Questions 20.17–18 refer to Questions 20.08–16.

Q20.17: In which of the Questions 20.08–16 would you expect that the relationship between the two variables could be represented by a straight-line graph passing through the origin?

Q20.18: In which of the straight-line graphs that pass through the origin (see Q20.17) do all the points on the line have meaning (not just the whole number values)?

For **Questions 20.19–20** use the squared paper provided at the end of this workbook to sketch a graph representing the linear relationship between temperatures in °F and in °C, given that 0°C is 32°F and 100°C is 212°F. To do this just plot the points (0, 32) and (100, 212), and join them with a straight line.

Q20.19: Use the graph to convert 82°F to °C; and to convert 16°C to °F.

Q20.20: How can you tell at a glance from the graph that these two units of temperature are not directly proportional?

Questions 20.21–32: Reasoning and problem solving (coordinates and linear relationships)

Questions 20.21–23 are about constructing a right-angled triangle ABC with two sides equal in length (in other words, a right-angled isosceles triangle). A is the point (1, 3) and B is the point (1, −1). Use the squared paper provided at the end of this workbook.

Q20.21: Give the coordinates of two possible positions for C in the first quadrant.

Q20.22: Give the coordinates of two possible positions for C in the second quadrant.

Q20.23: Give the coordinates of two possible positions for C in the third and fourth quadrants.

For **Questions 20.24–27** use the squared paper provided at the end of this workbook. Start by plotting these points and joining them up to form a rectangle: A (0, 0), B (4, 0), C (4, 3) and D (0, 3).

Q20.24: Now keep A and B fixed, but change C and D by adding 1 to each of their *x*-coordinates. What happens to the shape?

Q20.25: Starting with the result of Question 20.24 repeat the procedure of adding 1 to each of the *x*-coordinates of C and D to produce another shape. And then repeat the procedure again. This produces a sequence of parallelograms. What do they all have in common?

Q20.26: Find three possible positions for the fourth vertex of a parallelogram given that the other three vertices are (1, 1), (4, 2) and (4, 4).

Q20.27: Look at all the examples of parallelograms you have drawn in this question and find a rule that connects the *x*-coordinates of opposite vertices, and a rule that connects their *y*-coordinates.

Questions 20.28–32 are about latitude and longitude, which together are a special kind of coordinate system for locating points on the Earth's surface. For example, Kraków in Poland is on a latitude of 50° North and a longitude of 20° East (approximately). We could represent its location as (+50, +20).

Q20.28: Using this notation, Buenos Aires in Argentina is at (−35, −58). Explain what is meant by the two coordinates −35 and −58.

Q20.29: Where would you be at (0, 0)?

Q20.30: Where would you be at (90, 0), (90, 17) and (90, −42)?

Q20.31: Use an atlas or (better) a globe to identify a city located approximately at (+56, −3).

Q20.32: What would be the coordinates of a place on the globe diametrically opposite to the city identified in Question 20.31? Whereabouts is this place?

Questions 20.33–41: Learning and teaching (coordinates and linear relationships)

Questions 20.33–34 are about everyday examples that could be used to introduce younger children to the idea of a coordinate system.

Q20.33: Street maps are a familiar example of a simple coordinate system for identifying locations on a map. For example, on one page of a *London A–Z*, Harrow-on-the-Hill station is located in E2. Think of at least three other simple examples like this that you could use with children.

Q20.34: What particular feature of these simple everyday examples might be different from a Cartesian coordinate system and would require careful explanation to the children?

Questions 20.35–38 are about a mathematical game for two, three or four children; it can be adapted to various ages. Materials required are a grid as shown below and a set of cards numbered 1–24. The cards are shared equally between the children. They take turns to find a place to put one of their cards on the grid, no more than one card in each cell. Other players have to be convinced that the placement is correct! When they find they cannot play a card, they are out. The first player to get rid of all their cards or the player with the fewest cards left at the end is the winner.

	<12	even	odd	multiple of 3
multiple of 5				
>6				
factor of 30				
two digits				

Q20.35: A player has the card bearing the number 15. This could be placed in the square in the bottom right-hand corner, because it is both a multiple of 3 and a two-digit number. Where else could it be placed?

Q20.36: Which cards could be placed in the square in the bottom left-hand corner?

Q20.37: What is the value of this game in relation to understanding coordinates?

Q20.38: How could this game be adapted for younger children? For older children?

Questions 20.39–40 are about developing an activity involving some genuine mathematical thinking.

Q20.39: Start, for example, with the children plotting the points (0, 2), (0, 5), (5, 9) and (3, 0) and joining these up to form a non-rectangular quadrilateral. Do this yourself. Then reflect the quadrilateral (A) in the x-axis, by plotting the mirror image of each coordinate and joining them up to form a quadrilateral B. What are the coordinates of the vertices of quadrilateral B?

Q20.40: From this starting point, how might you develop an extended activity for children involving plotting coordinates to form shapes, reflections in the axes, the language 'same' and 'different', symmetry, reflections applied to reflections, and some real mathematical reasoning?

Question 20.41 asks you to reflect on the difference between teaching conventions and teaching concepts.

Q20.41: To use coordinates correctly, children have to learn the convention about which coordinate is given first (the horizontal or the vertical). What is the difference between a convention and a concept? How does learning a convention differ from understanding a concept in mathematics?

CONCEPTS AND PRINCIPLES OF MEASUREMENT

Questions related to Chapter 21 in *Mathematics Explained for Primary Teachers*, 7th edition.

Questions 21.01–20: Checking understanding (concepts and principles of measurement)

In **Questions 21.01–07** choose one of the options in the brackets to make the statement correct.

Q21.01: The quantity of water that a container can hold is called the (volume/capacity) of the container.

Q21.02: Both volume and capacity can be measured in (millimetres/litres).

Q21.03: The gravitational force that pulls an object downwards is called its (weight/mass).

Q21.04: The SI unit for measuring weight is the (newton/kilogram).

Q21.05: A kilogram is a measure of (mass/weight).

Q21.06: The (mass/weight) of an object does not change when its distance from the earth's centre changes.

Q21.07: Two different aspects of time are recorded time, such as (12:30 p.m./half an hour), and a time interval, such as (08:00/8 seconds).

In **Questions 21.08–09** complete the given statements about transitivity.

Q21.08: A mathematical relationship, represented by an arrow ($\rightarrow$), is transitive if the following is always the case: If A $\rightarrow$ B and B $\rightarrow$ C then ....

Q21.09:   If Ali is shorter than Ben and Ben is shorter than Carl, then Ali is ………

Questions 21.10–16 are some examples of relationships between members of the sets indicated in the brackets. Decide if each of these is transitive. If not, give a counter-example to demonstrate that the relationship is not transitive.

Q21.10:   'is taller than' {children in a class}

Q21.11:   'takes longer than' {activities planned by a teacher}

Q21.12:   'is twice as heavy as' {some objects on a table}

Q21.13:   'was born before' {children in a class}

Q21.14:   'is further from Birmingham than' {cities in the UK}

Q21.15:   'is nearer to Birmingham than it is to' {cities in the UK}

Q21.16:   'is a multiple of' {positive integers}

In each of **Questions 21.17–20**, put the four given items in order of size from the largest to the smallest.

Q21.17:   The length of your arm, 0.02 km, 15 inches, 15 cm.

Q21.18:   The mass of a small packet of crisps, 1200 mg, 0.5 kg, half a stone.

Q21.19:   The mass of half a litre of water, the mass of 500 ml of water, 0.5 kg, 500 g.

Q21.20:   The capacity of a can of soft drink, 0.75 litres, the volume of 2.5 kg of water, 80 ml.

Questions 21.21–30: Reasoning and problem solving (concepts and principles of measurement)

Questions 21.21–24 test your ability to estimate measurements. Try to do these questions without going online or using a calculator.

Q21.21:   In metres, estimate the height of a fully grown male giraffe.

Q21.22:   About how many days would it take to walk around the equator (if that were possible!) at the rate of 3 miles per hour non-stop? About 30 days? 100 days? 350 days? 4000 days?

Q21.23:   Estimate the mass in kilograms of a 10-litre bucket filled with sand.

Q21.24:   Roughly at what age would you reckon that children on average reach a height of one metre?

Questions 21.25–26 are about the concept of pressure in relation to weight.

Q21.25:   What would you say is the difference between pressure and weight?

Q21.26: Place a book in one hand, a 500-gram mass in the other and try to compare their weights. Can you be confident about which one is heavier and which one is lighter? Now place the two objects in identical plastic carrier bags and try again, holding on to the handles of the bags. Are you more confident now about which is heavier or lighter? If so, why do you think this might be?

Questions 21.27–28 are about the labelling of pre-packaged goods for sale in the European Union.

Q21.27: Pre-packaged supermarket goods bought in Europe show, next to the weight or volume indication, a symbol that looks like a slightly large lower-case letter 'e'. What is the meaning of this symbol?

Q21.28: A can of soft drink is labelled '330 ml e' and a large bottle is labelled '2 litres e'. Which would contain more of the drink? Six cans or one bottle?

Questions 21.29–30 provide a task that explores your abilities in mathematical reasoning in the context of weighing. First, an example:

You are given three masses, 20 g, 9 g and 5 g, a supply of sand and a balance with two pans, A and B. Your task is to measure out 24 g of sand in Pan B. You can do this by placing the 20 g and 9 g masses in Pan A and the 5 g mass in Pan B, and then pouring sand into Pan B until it balances Pan A.

Q21.29: You are given masses of 16 g, 7 g and 3 g and you want to measure out 12 g of sand in Pan B. To do this, you start by putting the 16-g mass in Pan A. How would you proceed?

Q21.30: Complete the table below to show which masses you would put in Pans A and B to measure out in Pan B the stated quantity of sand required, if you have available only the given masses in each row. The first row is the example given and the second row is the result of Question 21.29.

Masses available (g)	Mass of sand required (g)	Pan A	Pan B
20, 9, 5	24	20, 9	5
16, 7, 3	12		
2, 50, 40	12		
5, 55, 50	10		
14, 11, 3	6		
81, 7, 8	80		
55, 10, 5	60		
7, 6, 10	3		
30, 20, 8	18		
32, 20, 8	20		

Questions 21.31–44: Learning and teaching (concepts and principles of measurement)

In **Questions 21.31–32** some seven-year-old children are exploring weighing with a balance and some playdough.

Q21.31: The children take two lumps of playdough and place them in the two pans of a balance. One pan goes down and the other goes up. What conversation might you have with the children to develop their language and conceptual understanding in this context?

Q21.32: They now make two lumps of playdough that balance each other. How could you use this situation to give the children experience of conservation of mass? (Think of ways in which one of the lumps can be changed without changing its mass.)

Questions 21.33–35 provide examples of a teaching activity I call 'Grids'.

Q21.33: The task is to fill in the blank squares in the given grid, by writing down a time 25 minutes later in each square as you go from left to right, and 15 minutes earlier as you go down the columns. So, for example, the next entry in the top row is 11:00 a.m., and the next entry down in the first column is 10:20 a.m. Complete the grid. If you do this correctly, you should finish up with 11:25 a.m. in the bottom right-hand corner of the grid, whichever way you approach it. This is provided as a self-correcting element in the activity.

Q21.34: Suggest some other examples of grids like this that could be used in the context of 'time' and in other measuring contexts.

Q21.35: How might you practically incorporate this activity into your teaching of various measurement skills?

In **Questions 21.36–40** comment on the misunderstandings shown by the children and suggest how you might address them.

Q21.36: Six-year-old Liam measures the length of a pencil as 7 cm, using a tape measure as shown.

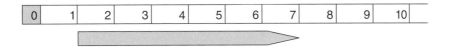

Q21.37: Seven-year-old Lou fills a small container with water and then pours this into a larger container. The teacher asks her which holds more water. Lou points to the smaller container, because 'this one was full, but that one is only half full'.

Q21.38: Jon, an eight-year-old, is asked which of the lines A and B is longer and replies that they are the same length.

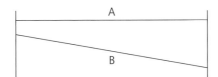

Q21.39: Jack, aged eight years, stood on one leg on the bathroom scales and read off 26 kg. Next, he stood on the other leg and again read off 26 kg. He then announced that this meant that he weighed 52 kg altogether!

Q21.40: Megan, aged nine years, estimates which is the heavier of a small, sealed box containing a 500-gram mass and a large lump of polystyrene (which is also about 500 grams). She is convinced that the small box is much heavier.

Questions 21.41–44 are some entertaining puzzles in various measurement contexts. Try these with older primary schoolchildren, when you have some odd moments to fill (if you ever do).

Q21.41: Atiano correctly makes the following assertions. 'The day before yesterday I was 10 years old. Next year I will have my 13th birthday.' What is the date when she is speaking and what is the date of her birthday?

Q21.42: You have an unmarked bottle that holds 3 litres when full and another one that holds 5 litres when full. How could you use these to measure out 4 litres, using no other containers?

Q21.43: In what context might you add 4 to 9 and get to 1?

Q21.44: In what context might you add 8 to 9 and get to 6?

PERIMETER, AREA AND VOLUME

Questions related to Chapter 22 in *Mathematics Explained for Primary Teachers*, 7th edition.

Questions 22.01–17: Checking understanding (perimeter, area and volume)

Questions 22.01–07 refer to the shapes shown below, made up of unit squares.

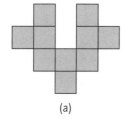
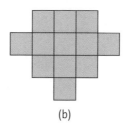
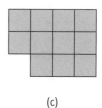

(a)   (b)   (c)

Q22.01: What is the area of shape (a)?

Q22.02: What is the perimeter of shape (b)?

Q22.03: Which of the shapes has the largest area?

Q22.04: Which of the shapes has the smallest area?

Q22.05: Which of the shapes has the greatest perimeter?

Q22.06: Which of the shapes has the smallest perimeter?

Q22.07: The 12 unit squares in shape (b) can be rearranged to make various shapes with the same area, but with different perimeters. What is the smallest possible perimeter that can be achieved?

Questions 22.08–11 are about conversions between different metric units of area and volume.

Q22.08:   What is the area of a square of side 0.6 m? Give your answer in square metres.

Q22.09:   Now answer Q22.08 in square centimetres.

Q22.10:   What is the volume of a cuboid 20 cm by 15 cm by 25 cm? Give your answer in cubic centimetres.

Q22.11:   Now answer Q22.10 in cubic metres.

Questions 22.12–14 are about plans to make a rectangular playground with a perimeter of 52 metres.

Q22.12:   If the playground is made 16 m long, how wide will it be? What will be the area?

Q22.13:   If the playground is made 4 m wide, how long will it be? What will be the area?

Q22.14:   What would be the dimensions of the playground with the largest area that could be made?

For **Questions 22.15–17** decide whether the statements are true or false.

Q22.15:   The length of a side of a square with an area of 0.16 m² is 0.8 m.

Q22.16:   Covering a square of side 0.25 m would require 25 cube blocks of side 0.05 m.

Q22.17:   If a cuboid-shaped container has internal edges of lengths 0.25 m, 0.5 m and 0.4 m, then 200 of these containers would be needed to store a cubic metre of sand.

Questions 22.18-29: Reasoning and problem solving (perimeter, area and volume)

Question 22.18 refers to the shapes shown below. Note that an isosceles triangle is a triangle with two equal sides.

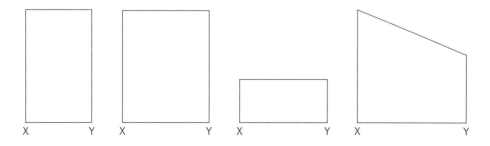

Q22.18: Inside each of these shapes, draw an isosceles triangle that has XY as one of the sides and the largest possible area.

Questions 22.19–20 are about parallelograms drawn on squared paper.

Q22.19: Draw a line 5 cm long along the bottom of a piece of cm-squared paper (provided at the end of this workbook). From one end, count up 3 cm and then 2 cm to the right and put a small cross. Do the same from the other end of the line. Join up the two crosses. Now join up the ends of the two 5-cm lines you have drawn. You should have a parallelogram.

Q22.20: Use the method shown in Chapter 22 of *Mathematics Explained* to cut up this parallelogram and transform it into a rectangle with the same height and base. What was the area of the parallelogram?

Questions 22.21–24 refer to the diagram shown below, which is a trapezium with a height of 10 cm and two parallel sides of lengths 12 cm and 6 cm. It has been sectioned into two right-angled triangles and a rectangle, all with the same height of 10 cm.

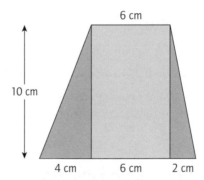

Q22.21: Use the composite shapes to find the area of this trapezium.

Q22.22: Repeat this with a trapezium of height 10 cm and two parallel sides of lengths 6 cm and 8 cm.

Q22.23: Do it again with a trapezium of height 10 cm and two parallel sides of 13 cm and 17 cm.

Q22.24: Complete the following rule: 'The area of a trapezium is the height multiplied by ...'.

For **Questions 22.25–29** you will need to study the diagram below (not drawn to scale), which shows how to make a box (with a lid) from a sheet of card whose dimensions are 30 cm × 21 cm. Ignoring flaps (which could be added later), you need to cut out the two shaded squares and the two shaded oblong rectangles, to leave the cross shape. Then fold this along the dotted lines to produce a box with a lid. The height of the box is h cm. This is the independent variable in this investigation. The dependent variable is the capacity of the box.

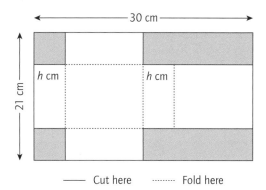

—— Cut here   ········ Fold here

Q22.25: If the height of the box is chosen to be 5 cm ($h = 5$), what would be the other two dimensions? What would be the capacity of this box?

Q22.26: If the height of the box is increased from 5 cm to 6 cm ($h = 6$), does that increase the capacity?

Q22.27: If $h = 4$ what is the capacity?

Q22.28: Using h cm for the height, what would be the other two dimensions?

Q22.29: What is the largest-capacity box you could make in this way from the given piece of card? With the help of a calculator or a spreadsheet, use a trial-and-improvement approach to solve this problem, working out the volume for various choices of height. Work to the nearest millimetre.

Questions 22.30–40: Learning and teaching (perimeter, area and volume)

For each of **Questions 22.30–32**, how would you interpret the child's error? Suggest ways of responding to the error.

Q22.30: A nine-year-old finds the perimeter of shape (b) in Q22.02 to be 8 units.

Q22.31: A ten-year-old, given that a rectangle has a perimeter of 48 cm and a width of 6 cm, calculates the length as 8 cm.

Q22.32: To find the area of the parallelogram shown below, an 11-year-old measures the lengths of the sides and gives the answer as 50 cm².

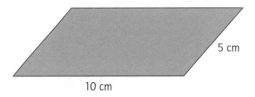

5 cm

10 cm

Questions 22.33–34 are about constructing assessment items based on the diagram below.

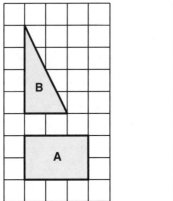 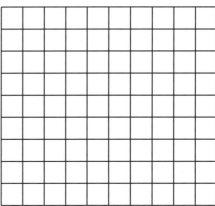

Q22.33: Produce a sequence of six questions, based on the above diagram, designed to assess children's increasing mastery of the concept of area. Question 1 (the easiest) and question 6 (the most challenging) are given. Your task is to write questions 2–5.

- Question 1: What is the area in square units of rectangle A?
- Question 6: On the grid on the right, draw a triangle half the area of triangle B.

Q22.34: What are some of the significant responses you might look out for to inform your teaching?

For **Questions 22.35–37** some children aged 10–11 years have a collection of cylindrical objects of different sizes. The teacher asks them to measure, to the nearest millimetre, the circumference and diameter of the circular cross-section of each object – and then to divide the circumference by the diameter, using a calculator.

Q22.35: Suggest two ways that children might measure the circumference.

Q22.36: Suggest two ways that children might measure the diameter.

Q22.37: What should the children discover and learn from this investigation?

Questions 22.38–40 relate to the diagram below. An 11-year-old is given four identical sheets of card, 24 cm by 26 cm: think of each sheet of card as being a 24-cm square with a 2-cm strip to act as a flap. These sheets of card are used to make four three-dimensional shapes as shown, with different cross-sections. Each shape is 24 cm high. The flap overlaps the opposite edge after folding and is glued in place.

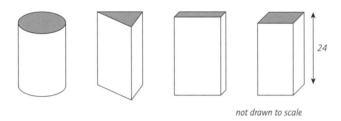

not drawn to scale

Q22.38: How would the child have to fold the sheets of card to produce the four three-dimensional shapes shown? These have the following cross-sections: (i) a circle with circumference 24 cm; (ii) an equilateral triangle of side 8 cm; (iii) a rectangle 2 cm by 10 cm; and (iv) a square of side 6 cm?

Q22.39: What are the perimeters of the cross-sections of these shapes?

Q22.40: Each of these card shapes in turn is then stood in an empty tray and filled to the brim with sand, making sure the shape is not distorted. Then the sand is let out into the tray and poured carefully into a measuring jug to find the volume of sand held by that shape. What would you expect the child to discover and learn from this experiment?

ANGLE

Questions related to Chapter 23 in *Mathematics Explained for Primary Teachers*, 7th edition.

Questions 23.01-18: Checking understanding (angle)

For each of the statements in **Questions 23.01–07**, decide whether it is always the case, sometimes the case or never the case. If sometimes, then give an example and a counter-example.

Q23.01: A quarter turn followed by another quarter turn about the same point is the same as a half turn.

Q23.02: A half turn followed by another half turn about the same point is equivalent to doing nothing.

Q23.03: The other two angles in a right-angled triangle are acute.

Q23.04: A quadrilateral has exactly two acute angles.

Q23.05: A quadrilateral has exactly three right angles.

Q23.06: A quadrilateral has two reflex angles.

Q23.07: One of the four angles in a quadrilateral is a reflex angle and one is an obtuse angle.

Question 23.08 refers to a 2-m long rigid metal pole. It is to be used as a lever to shift a heavy object.

Q23.08: The pivot is to be placed 50 cm from one end, as shown. This end would go under the object to be shifted. What angle does this end of the pole turn through when the other end is pulled downwards through an angle of 15°?

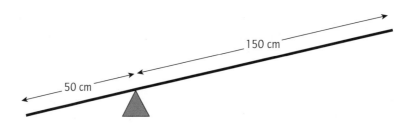

For **Questions 23.09–13** you need to remember that a regular two-dimensional shape is one in which all the sides are equal and all the angles are equal.

Q23.09: What is the size in degrees of each angle in a regular triangle (an equilateral triangle)?

Q23.10: What is the size in degrees of each angle in a regular quadrilateral (a square)?

Q23.11: What is the size in degrees of each angle in a regular five-sided figure (pentagon)?

Q23.12: What is the size in degrees of each angle in a regular six-sided figure (hexagon)?

Q23.13: What is the size in degrees of each angle in a regular seven-sided figure (heptagon)?

Questions 23.14–16 refer to the figure below (not drawn accurately).

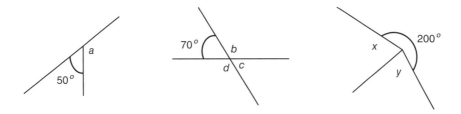

Q23.14: Calculate angle *a*.

Q23.15: Calculate angles *b*, *c* and *d*.

Q23.16: Given that angle *x* is equal to angle *y*, calculate angles *x* and *y*.

Questions 23.17–18 are about the external angles of a triangle.

Q23.17: Sketch a triangle PQR and label the internal angles as follows: angle P = 55°, angle Q = 38°. Work out the internal angle at R and label this. Now extend slightly the lines PQ, QR and RP, far enough to show the external angles at P, Q and R. Calculate what each of these external angles must be.

Q23.18: If a toy car drove along the three sides, PQ, QR and RP and back to where it started, turning through the external angle at each of the three vertices, what angle in total would it have turned through?

Questions 23.19-27: Reasoning and problem solving (angle)

For **Questions 23.19–20** you need to know that the latitude of London is about 51.5° North.

Q23.19: Through what angle would you turn if you travelled north from London to the North Pole?

Q23.20: Through what angle would you turn if you travelled south from London to the South Pole?

Question 23.21 relates to Questions 23.09–13.

Q23.21: All the shapes in Questions 23.09–13 are regular polygons. Generalize the results of those questions to give the size of the angles in degrees in a regular polygon with *n* sides.

Questions 23.22–24 are about two roads in the UK crossing each other at right angles at a roundabout.

Q23.22: You have driven up to the roundabout and taken the first exit. What angle has the car turned through?

Q23.23:   What angle has the car turned through if you have taken the third exit?

Q23.24:   What angle has the car turned through if you have gone round the round-about and back down the road you came along?

Questions 23.25–27 are some challenging problems about angles in a familiar context.

Q23.25:   Through what angles do the minute hand and the hour hand of a dial clock turn in 1 hour?

Q23.26:   What is the angle between the hour hand and the minute hand at 12:30 p.m.?

Q23.27:   To the nearest minute, at what times between 12 noon and 1 p.m. is the angle between the two hands a right angle?

Questions 23.28-34: Learning and teaching (angle)

Questions 23.28–30 provide some typical errors that children make with angles. Interpret these errors and suggest how you as a teacher would respond to them.

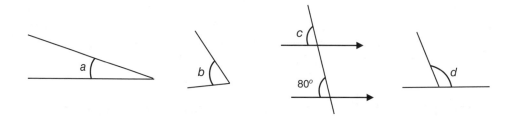

Q23.28:   Angle *a* is judged to be greater than angle *b*.

Q23.29:   Angle *c* is calculated as being 100°.

Q23.30:   Angle *d* is measured with a protractor as being 75°.

Questions 23.31–34 are about the provision of experiences of angle designed to help children develop their conceptual understanding.

Q23.31:   Make a list of examples of familiar experiences of turning something through an angle that could be used in discussion with young children in the early stages of introducing the concept of angle.

Q23.32:   Before introducing units for measuring angle, how could you give children practical experience of comparing and ordering angles using the static view of angle?

Q23.33: And how could you give children practical experience of comparing and ordering angles using the dynamic view of angle?

Q23.34: Devise a lesson for children aged 10–11 years based on the question, 'How good are the children in this class at estimating angle?' Assume the children have some experience of measuring angles in degrees using a protractor.

TRANSFORMATIONS AND SYMMETRY

Questions related to Chapter 24 in *Mathematics Explained for Primary Teachers*, 7th edition.

Questions 24.01-20: Checking understanding (transformations and symmetry)

In **Questions 24.01–11** decide whether the statement given is true or false.

Q24.01: A shape with reflective symmetry is its own mirror image.

Q24.02: A transformation is defined as a sliding from one position to another without turning.

Q24.03: When a shape is rotated clockwise through an angle of 50°, every straight line in the shape is rotated clockwise through an angle of 50°.

Q24.04: Two shapes are congruent if they differ only in position and orientation in space.

Q24.05: If two shapes are similar then one is a scaling of the other.

Q24.06: To scale up a shape we use a positive scale factor and to scale it down we use a negative scale factor.

Q24.07: A scaling by a factor of 0 would make a shape disappear.

Q24.08: A lower case d is a reflection of a lower case b.

Q24.09: A lower case p is a reflection of a lower case d.

Q24.10: Two mirror lines are at right angles to each other: reflecting a shape in one line and then reflecting the image in the other line is equivalent to rotating the shape through 180°.

Q24.11: A shape with rotational symmetry of order four must have four lines of symmetry.

For **Questions 24.12–17** refer to the diagram below. In identifying the transformations, be as specific as you can.

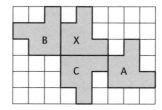

Q24.12:   Identify the transformation that maps shape X onto shape A.

Q24.13:   Identify the transformation that maps shape A onto shape X.

Q24.14:   Identify the transformation that maps shape X onto shape B.

Q24.15:   Identify the transformation that maps shape B onto shape X.

Q24.16:   Identify the transformation that maps shape X onto shape C.

Q24.17:   Identify the transformation that maps shape C onto shape X.

For **Questions 24.18–20** refer to the diagram below.

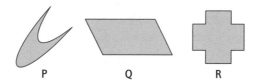

Q24.18:   Describe all the symmetries in shape P.

Q24.19:   Describe all the symmetries in shape Q.

Q24.20:   Describe all the symmetries in shape R.

Questions 24.21–30: Reasoning and problem solving (transformations and symmetry)

Question 24.21 is about recognizing equivalence between two shapes.

Q24.21:   The two diagrams shown below are obviously different from each other. But they are also the same in many respects. Make a list of as many ways as you can think of in which they are the same. Write sentences beginning with 'They both …' or 'they are both …'. Be creative!

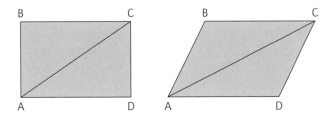

Questions 24.22–24 investigate the result of successive reflections in two parallel mirror lines.

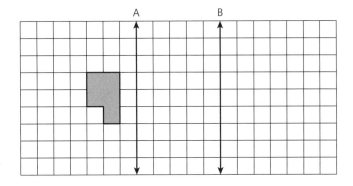

Q24.22: The mirror lines A and B are 5 units apart. The object shown is reflected first in A and then the image is reflected in B. What single transformation is equivalent to this?

Q24.23: Explore what happens for various starting positions for the object being reflected. What happens, for example, when the object is between the two mirror lines?

Q24.24: Try this with the parallel mirror lines a different distance apart. Can you articulate a generalization?

Questions 24.25–29 are about the A paper sizes (in particular, A3, A4 and A5). These are all mathematically similar. A sheet of A4 paper is a scaling up of a sheet of A5 paper in such a way that the area is doubled: two sheets of A5 make a sheet of A4. A3 has the same relationship to A4. The following questions will help with enlarging and reducing on a photocopier. You may need to use a calculator for some parts of the questions.

Q24.25: How many sheets of A5 make a sheet of A3?

Q24.26: Scaling by what factor would transform A5 into A3?

Q24.27: Scaling by what factor would transform A5 into A4 and A4 into A3?

Q24.28: Scaling by what factor would transform A3 into A5?

Q24.29: Scaling by what factor would transform A3 into A4 and A4 into A5?

Question 24.30 is an intriguing conundrum about reflections in our everyday experience.

Q24.30: If you look in a mirror, your reflection has your left and right reversed. So, for example, if you raise your right hand the person in the mirror raises their left hand. Why does the mirror not reverse top and bottom? Are there circumstances in which a mirror does reverse top and bottom?

Questions 24.31–39: Learning and teaching (transformations and symmetry)

Questions 24.31–33 are about children exploring symmetry. For each question, assume the children have access to a set of various plastic 2-dimensional shapes.

Q24.31: Name some of the shapes that you would want to include to ensure there are examples of shapes with: (a) both reflective and rotational symmetry; (b) reflective symmetry but not rotational; (c) rotational symmetry but not reflective; (d) neither rotational symmetry nor reflective.

Q24.32: Suggest two different ways that the children can practically test whether or not a shape has reflective symmetry.

Q24.33: Suggest two different ways that the children can practically test whether or not a shape has rotational symmetry.

Questions 24.34–35 refer to the diagram below. This is a typical assessment item for Key Stage 2 children.

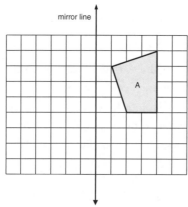

Q24.34:   'Draw the position of quadrilateral A after it has been reflected in the mirror line.' What are the key ideas or procedures you would emphasize with children to help them answer this kind of question?

Q24.35:   'Draw the position of quadrilateral A after it has been translated +2 units in the horizontal direction and −3 units in the vertical direction.' What are the key ideas or procedures you would emphasize with children to help them answer this kind of question?

The activity for **Questions 24.36–39** is just a delightful experience for you to share with children. But first you have to experience it yourself. Sit at a table in a well-lit area. You need two small rectangular mirrors and an A4 sheet of paper with a bold straight line drawn across it. Put the two mirrors at an angle of about 120° across the line as shown and look into them. Adjust the position of the mirrors until the line on the paper and the images in the two mirrors form an equilateral triangle. Now slowly make the angle between the mirrors smaller until the line on the paper and the images in the mirror form a square.

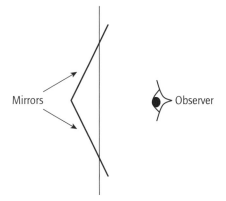

Q24.36:   What is the angle between the mirrors when what you can see is a square?

Q24.37:   Continue making the angle smaller, to produce a regular pentagon and then a regular hexagon. What is the angle between the mirrors when what you can see is a regular hexagon?

Q24.38:   If you continue making the angle smaller, you should be able to see a regular heptagon, a regular octagon and so on. How many lines of symmetry do the shapes in this whole sequence have?

Q24.39:   What happens when the angle between the mirrors gets really small?

CLASSIFYING SHAPES

Questions related to Chapter 25 in *Mathematics Explained for Primary Teachers*, 7th edition.

Questions 25.01–17: Checking understanding (classifying shapes)

For each of **Questions 25.01–10**, decide whether the statement about two-dimensional shapes is true or false.

Q25.01: All rhombuses are parallelograms.

Q25.02: A square is not necessarily a rhombus.

Q25.03: If a parallelogram has two lines of symmetry, then it must be a rhombus.

Q25.04: All equilateral triangles are also isosceles.

Q25.05: A triangle may contain both a right angle and an obtuse angle.

Q25.06: A square is not a rectangle.

Q25.07: The diagonals of any rectangle bisect each other (cut each other in half, exactly).

Q25.08: Any hexagon will tessellate.

Q25.09: A regular pentagon has exactly five lines of symmetry.

Q25.10: A circle is a two-dimensional shape with one side.

For each of **Questions 25.11–17**, decide whether the statement about three-dimensional shapes is true or false.

Q25.11: All the faces of a regular tetrahedron are equilateral triangles.

Q25.12: A cube is not a cuboid.

Q25.13: A cylinder has three faces.

Q25.14: A cube can be constructed from two square-based pyramids.

Q25.15: An octagonal prism has 8 rectangular faces and 2 octagonal faces.

Q25.16: A regular dodecahedron has 12 identical faces and 30 edges all the same length.

Q25.17: A sphere is a three-dimensional shape with one face.

Questions 25.18-32: Reasoning and problem solving (classifying shapes)

For **Questions 25.18–21** you will need to refer to a website or book that shows the flags of the world. In answering this question, ignore the colours and symbols used in the flags. Focus just on the shapes in the design.

Q25.18: Find a country beginning with A whose flag is a rectangle divided into an isosceles triangle and two right-angled triangles.

Q25.19: Find two countries beginning with M whose flag is a rectangle divided in two by a line of symmetry.

Q25.20: Find a country beginning with C whose flag is a rectangle divided into an isosceles triangle and two trapeziums.

Q25.21: Find a Republic beginning with C whose flag is a rectangle containing two right-angled triangles with a parallelogram between them.

Questions 25.22–24 relate to a block of cheese that is a prism with a square cross-section, as shown.

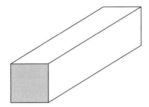

Q25.22: By making one slice with a sharp knife, how could you cut off a piece of this cheese that is a cube?

Q25.23: By making one slice with a sharp knife, how could you cut off a piece of this cheese that is a triangular prism?

Q25.24: By making one slice with a sharp knife, how could you cut off a piece of this cheese that is a tetrahedron?

Questions 25.25–26 are about using two-dimensional nets to make three-dimensional shapes.

Q25.25: Of which three-dimensional shapes are X, Y and Z nets?

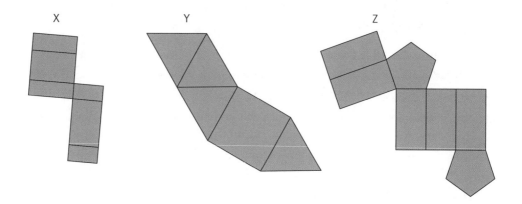

Q25.26:   Which of P, Q, R and S is *not* the net of a cuboid?

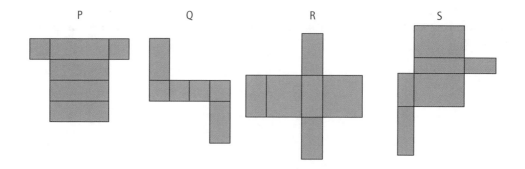

Questions 25.27–28 are two challenging little problems that require some creative thinking.

Q25.27   Draw a triangle cut by a single straight line, so that the resulting diagram contains three obtuse-angled triangles.

Q25.28:   Draw a quadrilateral cut by a single straight line, so that the resulting diagram contains four triangles.

Questions 25.29–32 provide an example of how a sequence of geometric shapes can be used to explore number patterns and to give opportunities for articulating generalizations. Consider the sequence of tessellations shown below. The starting shape is a black trapezium tile. The first expansion of this is produced by surrounding it with identical grey tiles; and the second expansion by surrounding the first expansion with more black tiles; and so on.

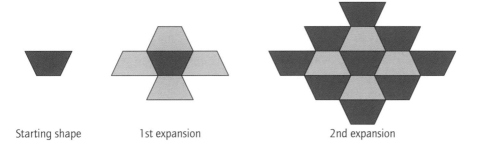

Starting shape   1st expansion   2nd expansion

Q25.29: How many grey tiles have to be added to make the third expansion?

Q25.30: How many black tiles have then to be added to make the fourth expansion?

Q25.31: How many tiles altogether are needed to make the tenth expansion of the tessellation?

Q25.32: Which of these formulas gives the total number of tiles needed to make the nth expansion?

(a) $8n - 3$ (b) $4n + 1$ (c) $2n(n + 1) + 1$ (d) $4n^2 + 1$

Questions 25.33–40: Learning and teaching (classifying shapes)

Questions 25.33–36 contain some common errors made about shapes.

Q25.33: A six-year-old insists that a square drawn with its sides at an angle of 45 degrees to the edges of the page is a diamond and not a square. How would you respond?

Q25.34: A seven-year-old calls a sphere a circle and a cube a square. How would you respond?

Q25.35: A ten-year-old says that the diagonals of a parallelogram are lines of symmetry. How would you respond?

Q25.36: The National Curriculum for Mathematics in England requires Year 5 children to 'calculate and compare the area of rectangles (including squares) … and estimate the area of irregular shapes'. What mathematical error is implicit in this statement?

Question 25.37 relates to a lesson on shape with some able children aged 10–11 years.

Q25.37: The teacher had demonstrated to the children that there were only five regular polyhedra. Then one of the children stuck together two regular tetrahedra and told the teacher he had discovered another one, with six faces, all of which were identical equilateral triangles. How might the teacher respond to this?

Questions 25.38–40 relate to an activity with two-dimensional shapes suitable for a whole-class discussion. Using a graphical display feature (for example, the Draw feature on a computer or whiteboard), draw a two-dimensional shape. Using the scroll bar, gradually reveal the shape on the screen, asking the children to deduce what they think the shape is going to be from the visible features revealed at any stage. For example, the sequence below shows a square being gradually revealed.

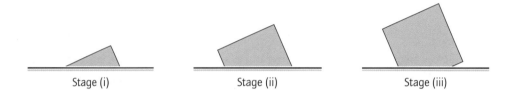

Stage (i)   Stage (ii)   Stage (iii)

Q25.38: At stage (i), several children say that the shape must be a triangle. At stage (ii), they change their minds and say that it is a rectangle. At stage (iii), many are now convinced that it is a square. What questions might the teacher use effectively at each of these stages?

Q25.39: Suggest some other shapes that could be used in this activity to promote mathematical reasoning.

Q25.40: Write a specific learning objective for this activity.

HANDLING DATA

Questions related to Chapter 26 in *Mathematics Explained for Primary Teachers*, 7th edition.

Questions 26.01–12: Checking understanding (handling data)

For **Questions 26.01–03** explain the difference between …

Q26.01: … a block graph and a bar chart;

Q26.02: … a discrete variable and a continuous variable;

Q26.03: … a simple pictogram and a block graph.

For **Questions 26.04–05** some children have collected data about how many numbered pages there are in a sample of 100 books taken randomly from the school library. The smallest number of pages is 64 and the largest is 312.

Q26.04: Is this data continuous or discrete?

Q26.05: How best might the data be organized and presented in graphical form?

Questions 26.06–08 refer to a tally chart that is being compiled to show the numbers of children in a year group with birthdays in the four quarters of the year. There are 100 children in total in the year group. The tally chart shown below is incomplete. To be added to this chart are 4 more children in the first quarter, 2 more in the second quarter, 3 more in the third quarter, and the rest in the fourth quarter.

Jan–Mar	ꟷꟷꟷ ꟷꟷꟷ ꟷꟷꟷ ꟷꟷꟷ ꟷꟷꟷ
Apr–Jun	ꟷꟷꟷ ꟷꟷꟷ ꟷꟷꟷ ꟷꟷꟷ
Jul–Sep	ꟷꟷꟷ ꟷꟷꟷ ꟷꟷꟷ ꟷꟷꟷ ꟷꟷꟷ
Oct–Dec	ꟷꟷꟷ ꟷꟷꟷ ꟷꟷꟷ

Q26.06: Complete the tally chart.

Q26.07: Compile a frequency table for this data.

Q26.08: Draw a bar chart for this data.

Questions 26.09–12 are about data collected for 300 children in a primary school, recording (a) the month and year in which they were born (for example, March 2015); and (b) the season (spring, summer, autumn, winter) in which their birthday falls.

Q26.09: Why would a pie chart be an appropriate way of representing the number of children born in each of the four seasons?

Q26.10: If 100 children were born in the autumn, what would be the angle in the pie chart for this sector?

Q26.11: Why would a pie chart be an inappropriate way of representing the data about 'month and year of birth'?

Q26.12: How could the data about month and year of birth be represented graphically?

Questions 26.13–17: Reasoning and problem solving (handling data)

Questions 26.13–14 are two examples of data handling in surveys.

Q26.13:   An advertisement for a chain of coffee shops declares: '7 out of 10 coffee lovers prefer our coffee.' The small print on the poster explains how this conclusion was reached. What information would you require in this small print to convince you that their claim is justified?

Q26.14:   In a survey, 1000 teachers were asked whether or not they approved of the government's latest education initiative. They could answer yes, no or undecided. What is wrong with the following bar chart showing the results of this survey? In what way is it misleading?

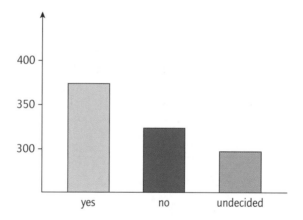

Questions 26.15–17 refer to the data in the table below, which shows how many primary teacher trainees in a cohort had various numbers of A levels (excluding any equivalent level 3 or higher qualifications).

Number of A levels	0	1	2	3	4
Number of trainees	5	12	42	23	8

Q26.15:   How many trainees were there in this cohort?

Q26.16:   To one decimal place, what percentage of trainees had 2 or more A levels?

Q26.17:   Enter the data in the table into a computer spreadsheet (such as an Excel spreadsheet). Get the computer to produce a pie chart for this data, looking like the one shown below. If necessary, get a computer buff to help you.

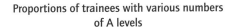

Proportions of trainees with various numbers
of A levels

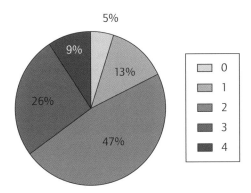

Questions 26.18-30: Learning and teaching (handling data)

Questions 26.18–20 provide a simple structure for giving children data about themselves, organized according to two variables.

Q26.18: Give two examples of questions to which each child in a class could answer only yes or no.

Q26.19: How do the answers to your two questions divide the class up into four subsets?

Q26.20: Suggest two ways in which the children might represent these four subsets in one diagram?

For **Questions 26.21–23** assume that you are planning a cross-curricular project on transport for a class of children aged 10–11 years. Think about the kind of data that is suggested in each question and how you could use this to develop key skills in handling data and representing it in graphical form.

Q26.21: How might you use data that shows a gradual increase as children get older in the percentages of children who regularly cycle to school?

Q26.22: How might you use data about the approximate distances in kilometres that the children in a particular year group travel to school?

Q26.23: How might you use the responses of parents of children in a school in Norwich to the following question: if you won a week's holiday for two in a hotel in Edinburgh, how would you choose to travel there?

Questions 26.24–25 are two examples of children using particular kinds of graphical representation of data inappropriately.

Q26.24: A child collects data from the class about their favourite from a list of six fruits and presents it in a line graph as shown. How would you help the child to realize why this is an inappropriate way of presenting this data? How would it be presented more appropriately?

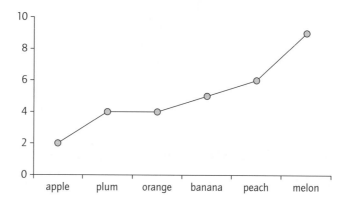

Q26.25: A child does a survey of how many children in a class of 30 have visited various local attractions. The child discovers that 10 children have visited the local zoo, 12 have visited the nearest theme park, 5 have visited the town theatre, 5 have visited the town concert hall and 28 have visited a particular beach. The data is put into a spreadsheet and turned into a pie chart, as shown below. What's wrong with this?

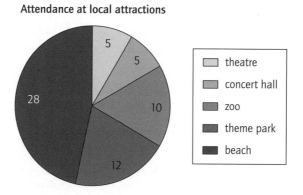

Attendance at local attractions

For **Questions 26.26–29** refer to the simple scatter diagram shown. This is used to represent data about how many boys and how many girls there are in the families of 30 children in a class.

Q26.26: How many families had 1 girl and 1 boy?

Q26.27: How many families had more than 2 boys?

Q26.28: How many families had 2 children?

Q26.29: Using lots of different ideas, make a list of questions you could ask the children to be answered from this diagram. Answer your own questions. Be creative!

For **Question 26.30** imagine that you are planning to teach some children how to group data for a discrete numerical variable (such as the number of letters in the sentences in a chapter of a book) and to represent the data in a simple bar chart.

Q26.30: Write a list of specific learning objectives to make clear to you and the children what they should be able to do at the end of the lessons on this topic. Here's one to get you started:

'The children should be able to decide when a set of data for a discrete numerical variable should be grouped into intervals for the purposes of drawing a bar chart.'

COMPARING SETS OF DATA

Questions related to Chapter 27 in *Mathematics Explained for Primary Teachers*, 7th edition.

Questions 27.01-17: Checking understanding (comparing sets of data)

Questions 27.01–09 refer to the data in the frequency table, which shows how many of the chapters in a book occupied various numbers of pages.

Number of pages	7	8	9	10	11	12	13	14	15	16	17	18
Number of chapters	1	3	2	3	2	4	5	3	1	1	1	1

Q27.01: What is the total number of chapters in the book?

Q27.02: What is the total number of pages occupied by these chapters?

Q27.03: What is the modal number of pages per chapter?

Q27.04: What is the minimum numbers of pages per chapter?

Q27.05: What is the maximum numbers of pages per chapter

Q27.06: What is the range of the number of pages per chapter?

Q27.07: What is the median number of pages per chapter?

Q27.08: To one decimal place, what is the mean number of pages per chapter?

Q27.09: Complete this sentence, used to compare this book with other books: 'The chapters are quite short: typically there are about … or … pages per chapter.

Questions 27.10–15 refer to the five-number summaries for two primary schools, A and B, showing the performance of their Year 6 children in an IQ test.

	Minimum	LQ	Median	UQ	Maximum
School A	84	92	101	112	115
School B	72	86	102	120	132

Q27.10: School A had 95 children in Year 6. How would the median score have been obtained?

Q27.11: What do LQ and UQ stand for? How would these have been obtained for School A?

Q27.12: What can you say about the scores of the top 25% of children in School B?

Q27.13: What can you say about the scores of the bottom 25% children in School B?

Q27.14: Compare the medians and the inter-quartile ranges for the two schools. What does this comparison tell you about their respective performances in the test?

Q27.15: When the scores for the two schools were combined into one list, the scores at the 5th and 95th percentile were 81 and 124. What do these statistics tell you?

For **Questions 27.16–17** refer to the diagram, which shows the proportions of numbers of reference books (R), educational books (E) and fiction books (F) sold by a bookshop and a supermarket in a week.

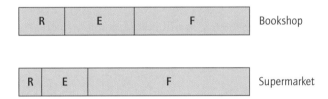

Q27.16: If the bookshop sold a total of 400 books, estimate the actual numbers of books in each category that the bookshop sold.

Q27.17: If the supermarket sold a total of 250, estimate the actual numbers of books in each category that the supermarket sold.

Questions 27.18-28: Reasoning and problem solving (comparing sets of data)

For **Questions 27.18–21** you are told that the mean ages of children in the three Year 4 classes in a junior school are 8.85 years, 8.54 years and 8.38 years, calculated to two decimal places.

Q27.18: Must it be true that the mean age of the whole year group, calculated to two decimal places, is less than 8.85 years?

Q27.19: Must it be true that the mean age of the whole year group, calculated to two decimal places, is more than 8.38 years?

Q27.20: Must it be true that the mean age of the whole year group, calculated to two decimal places, is (8.85 + 8.54 + 8.38) ÷ 3 = 8.59 years?

Q27.21: Must it be true that half the children in the year group are 8.54 years or older?

Questions 27.22–24 provide an opportunity for some pure mathematical reasoning. For these questions you need to know that a sequence of numbers in which the difference between successive terms is constant is called an arithmetic sequence.

Q27.22: As an example, 3, 7, 11, 15, 19 is an arithmetic sequence. This is because the difference between successive terms is always 4. Find the mean and the median of the five numbers in this sequence.

Q27.23: Here is another arithmetic sequence: 7, 10, 13, 16, 19, 22. The difference between successive terms is 3. Find the mean and the median of the six numbers in this sequence.

Q27.24: Try this for other sets of numbers that form an arithmetic sequence and discover something interesting about the median and the mean.

Questions 27.25–28 may challenge your understanding of average speed!

Q27.25: On a car journey of 400 miles, I average a speed of 40 miles per hour. How long does the journey take?

Q27.26: On the way back, I average a speed of 50 miles per hour. How long does the return journey take?

Q27.27: What is the average speed for the whole journey, there and back?

Q27.28: On another day, for an outward journey of 100 miles, I averaged 20 miles per hour. What average speed is required on the return journey to give an overall average speed of 40 miles per hour?

Questions 27.29-36: Learning and teaching (comparing sets of data)

Questions 27.29–31 relate to an item proposed for an end of Year 6 mathematics assessment.

Q27.29: Consider this set of numbers: {3, 3, 3, 4, 5, 5, 6, 7, 8, 8}. What is the mode for this set of numbers?

Q27.30: What is the range for this set of numbers?

Q27.31: Questions 27.29 and 27.30 are proposed as an assessment item. Criticize them!

Questions 27.32–34 are about a transport project, in which some children plan to compare the Year 6 children in their urban school with the Year 6 children in a rural school. They want to compare (a) how the two year groups travel to school (bus, walk, bicycle, car), and (b) how many minutes, approximately, it takes them to get to school. How would you help the children to plan this project?

Q27.32: What data should they collect and how should it be organized?

Q27.33: What statistics might they use to make comparisons?

Q27.34: How might you encourage them to present their findings graphically to show the comparisons most clearly?

Questions 27.35–36 relate to the teacher's need to interpret statistical data in their professional role.

	Minimum	LQ	Median	UQ	Maximum
Test A	42	56	68	82	92
Test B	58	69	80	90	100

Q27.35: The table above is derived from the results of 200 Year 4 children who took two mathematics assessments, Tests A and B, with marks out of 100. What comparisons can you make between the two tests?

Q27.36: Which of the assessments generated the more desirable set of results from the teacher's perspective? To answer this, think about the purposes that teachers might have in assessing children.

PROBABILITY

Questions related to Chapter 28 in *Mathematics Explained for Primary Teachers*, 7th edition.

Questions 28.01-18: Checking understanding (probability)

Use **Questions 28.01–06** to assess your basic understanding of probability.

Q28.01: What does it mean to say that the chances of an event occurring are evens?

Q28.02: What is the meaning of assigning an event a probability of zero?

Q28.03: Three conventional dice are thrown and the sum of the numbers shown is calculated. Give an example of an outcome with a probability of zero.

Q28.04:   What is the meaning of assigning an event a probability of 1?

Q28.05:   Three conventional dice are thrown and the sum of the numbers shown is calculated. Give an example of an outcome with a probability of 1.

Q28.06:   What everyday language would you associate with probabilities of 0.01, 0.15, 0.85 and 0.99?

For **Questions 28.07–09** decide what would be the best way to determine the probability described.

Q28.07:   The probability that the side batting last in a test match at the Oval cricket ground in Kennington will reach a total of 500 or more to win the match.

Q28.08:   The probability of scoring less than 5 when throwing a conventional die.

Q28.09:   The probability of a person choosing 7 when asked to choose a number less than 10.

Questions 28.10–18 are about simultaneously tossing a coin and a conventional six-faced die.

Q28.10:   List all the possible outcomes of someone simultaneously tossing a coin and throwing a die. (For example, one outcome might be H5, a head and a five.)

Q28.11:   What is the probability that the outcome is T3?

Q28.12:   What is the probability of getting a tail and an even number?

Q28.13:   What is the probability of getting a head and an odd number?

Q28.14:   Are the events in Questions 28.11 and 28.12 mutually exclusive?

Q28.15:   What is the probability of getting either a tail and an even number or a head and an odd number?

Q28.16:   What is the probability of getting a tail and a number less than 5?

Q28.17:   What is the probability of getting a tail and either an even number or a number less than 5?

Q28.18:   Why is the answer to Question 28.17 not equal to the sum of the answers to Questions 28.12 and 28.16?

Questions 28.19–30: Reasoning and problem solving (probability)

Questions 28.19–23 are about a six-faced die that has two blue faces, two red faces and two yellow faces.

Q28.19:   When the die is thrown once, what is the probability that the uppermost face will be yellow?

Q28.20: If I then throw this die again, is the outcome independent of what happened on the first throw?

Q28.21: What is the probability that both throws will result in the uppermost face being yellow?

Q28.22: If I plan to throw the die six times in succession, what is the probability that I will get yellow on all six throws?

Q28.23: If I have thrown the die 10 times and got yellow every time, what is the probability of getting yellow on the next throw?

Questions 28.24–26 are an opportunity to test your intuition about probability.

Q28.24: Twelve books written in English are taken at random off a library shelf. For each book you turn to page 50. How likely do you feel it is that in at least two of these books the first word on page 50 will begin with the same letter? Answer with a phrase like 'very unlikely' or 'fairly likely', or estimate a numerical probability.

Q28.25: A pack of 52 playing cards contains 13 'spades'. Someone shuffles the pack and draws a card apparently at random and predicts that it will be a spade. It is a spade. They do this again and draw another spade. And again. How many times would this happen before you would be convinced that they were cheating?

Q28.26: A die is thrown six times. Which of the following three outcomes do you think is most likely and which do you think is least likely? (a) Scoring 1, 2, 3, 4, 5, 6 in that order. (b) Scoring 6 every time. (c) Scoring 2, 5, 1, 3, 3, 6 in that order.

Questions 28.27–29 will test your mathematical reasoning about probability. You are told that the probability of a 50-year-old male teacher in England being alive on his 70th birthday is 0.8 and the probability of his being alive on his 80th birthday is 0.5.

Q28.27: Are these two events independent?

Q28.28: Are they mutually exclusive?

Q28.29: What is the probability of both these events occurring?

Question 28.30 is about an advertisement for a slimming product that I spotted in a well-known store.

Q28.30: The advertisement claims that the product will 'increase your chances of losing weight by 50%'. Have you any idea what this might mean?

Questions 28.31–38: Learning and teaching (probability)

For **Questions 28.31–33** each child in a class of 30 throws two dice 20 times and records the frequencies of scores from 2 to 12.

Q28.31: Before the data is collected and compiled, you ask the class which score they would expect to occur most often. How would you discuss this with the class?

Q28.32: You also ask them which score they would expect to occur least often. How would you discuss this with the class?

Q28.33: How could you use the data collected here to develop some understanding of key ideas of probability and sampling?

Questions 28.34–38 provide an opportunity to design a probability investigation for children aged 10–11 years. Questions 28.34–37 describe four events. For each of these events, suggest how you could plan for children to collect data in order to estimate the probability of the event occurring.

Q28.34: When asked to name a vegetable, a child in our school replies 'carrot'.

Q28.35: Three conventional dice are thrown and at least two of the numbers that come up are the same.

Q28.36: You turn to a page of a book at random and the first line of text contains the word 'the'.

Q28.37: You choose 'stone' and then 'paper' alternately when playing ten rounds of the 'stone, paper, scissors' game and you win more rounds than you lose.

Q28.38: Now suggest how you might build the investigation of these probabilities into an extended activity to explore the children's intuitive sense of probability, to develop the language of probability and to promote their mastery of the mathematics of probability.

SOLUTIONS AND NOTES

6.01: If you saw this as a set of six, without counting, you have demonstrated the skill of *subitizing*.

6.02: Real numbers

6.03: Natural numbers

6.04: Rational numbers

6.05: Integers

6.06: 42,076 (forty-two thousand and seventy-six)

6.07: 7,000,653 (seven million, six hundred and fifty-three)

6.08: 50,000,000 (fifty million)

6.09: £7000

6.10: £7100

6.11: £7100

6.12: £7099

6.13: DCCLXVIII (768)

6.14: CDXCIX (499)

6.15: 620 (CCCLXXVIII is 378)

6.16: 1 large cube and 5 units; equivalent to 1005 units.

6.17: Count on 1 from 2,069,999 and you get to 2,070,000.

6.18: Count back 1 from 4,980,000 and you get to 4,979,999.

6.19: Count on by 10 from 3,090,990 and you get to 3,091,000.

6.20: Count back by 10 from 1,500,005 and you get to 1,499,995.

6.21: (a) Four. (b) Forty. (c) Il n'y a pas de chiffres en français pour les questions (a) et (b).

6.22: To represent the whole numbers from 0 to 99, you need the ten cards with single digits on them (0, 1, 2, 3, … 9), plus a further 9 cards with the multiples of 10 from 10 to 90 on them; so 19 cards in total. To represent the whole numbers from 0 to 999, you need these 19 cards plus a further 9 cards with the multiples of 100 from 100 to 900 on them; so 28 in total. To represent the whole numbers from 0 to 9999, you need these 28 cards plus a further 9 cards with the multiples of 1000 from 1000 to 9000 on them; so 37 in total.

6.23: The next numbers after 27, 37, 77 and 277 are 30, 40, 100 and 300, respectively. When you add one to a seven, in base eight, the eight you get is exchanged for another one in the next position to the left: 'eight of these are exchanged for one of these'.

6.24: The numeral 35 in base eight means 3 *eights* and 5 ones, which equals 29 in base ten.

6.25: The 4-times table in base eight is 4, 10, 14, 20, 24, 30, 34, 40 and so on. This has the same pattern as the 5-times table in base ten. This is because just as two fives make ten, so do two fours make eight.

6.26: The 7-times table in base eight is 7, 16, 25, 34, 43, 52, 61, 70 and so on. This has the same pattern as the 9-times table in base ten. This is because just as nine is one less than ten, so is seven one less than eight.

6.27: 101 (CI), 105 (CV), 110 (CX)

6.28: 103 (CIII), 104 (CIIII), 107 (CVII)

6.29: 102 (CII), 106 (CVI), 111 (CXI)

6.30: The sequence of 100 numbers beginning with 301 (CCCI).

6.31: Some suggestions for the display: the word 'four'; several examples of the numeral '4' cut out from magazines or newspapers; a number strip with square 4 highlighted; a birthday card for a four-year-old; a photograph of four children; a picture of a house with number 4 on the door; a number 4 bus; the counting numbers, 1, 2, 3, 4, 5, 6 and so on, with 4 highlighted; a photograph of Class 4; a square; a hand holding up four fingers; four coloured counters; four pence and a shop label saying '4p'; pictures of an animal with four legs and a table with four legs; the question, 'how many letters in "four"?' (See Q6.21(a) solution above.)

6.32: In counting, children find 'the number before' a much more difficult idea than 'the next number', because, of course, they count up much more than they count down. Ask the child to stand on a square on a number strip in the playground, then to walk backwards along it, each time predicting the number they will step on. Play games on a number strip that uses the words 'before' and 'next', with instructions like 'go to the number before this one'.

6.33: This probably arises because the child incorrectly connects the symbols '00' with the word 'hundred'. The child has to learn that it is just the 3 in 300 that says '3 hundred' (because of its position) and the two zeros tell you that you have no tens and no zeros. Make the connection with coins or base-ten blocks. Use arrow cards, as shown, to help establish the idea, for example, that 324 is made from 300, 20 and 4.

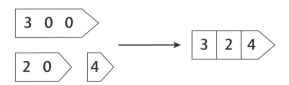

6.34: The child's error is probably related to the fact that when you say 'three thousand and ninety-nine' the zero is not mentioned; plus the fact that such big numbers are not in their everyday experience of counting. Give the child examples like this to do using the base-ten blocks shown in Question 6.16, putting out, say, 3 blocks, 9 longs and 9 units, then adding one more unit, and exchanging.

6.35: Ask an individual volunteer to state which number comes between the other two and then invite the child to *convince* you. Ensure that the phrases '41 is greater than 39' and '41 is less than 60' are articulated. Repeat with other sets of three numbers.

6.36: Two examples of objectives:

a   Given a handful of 1p and 10p coins to reduce this to the smallest number of equivalent coins, using a process of exchanging 'ten of these for one of those'.

b   Given a collection of base-ten units and tens, to reduce this to the smallest number of equivalent blocks, using a process of exchanging 'ten of these for one of those'.

6.37: Two examples of objectives:

a   To say in words the name of any written three-digit numeral.

b   To demonstrate the meaning of the digits in a three-digit number by selecting appropriate coins from a supply of 1p, 10p and pound coins.

6.38: Two examples of objectives:

a   To indicate the approximate position of any three-digit number, given either in words or as a numeral, on a number line marked in hundreds.

b   To say (in words) and write (as a numeral) the approximate number corresponding to a given point on a number line marked in hundreds.

6.39: Two examples of objectives:

    a   To arrange a set of numbers (up to, say, 9999) in order from smallest to largest, or from largest to smallest.

    b   To say and write a number that comes between two given numbers (up to, say, 9999).

6.40: Aim to place cards with larger-value digits (9, 8, 7, 6) in your hundreds boxes and those with smaller-value digits (0, 1, 2, 3, 4) in an opponent's hundreds. If your hundreds are full, put the greater digits in your tens boxes. If an opponent's hundreds boxes are full, put smaller digits in their tens boxes.

6.41: The game focuses attention on the place value of the digits in a three-digit number. For example, a 9 is worth 900 if placed in the first box, but only 90 in the second box, and merely 9 in the third box.

6.42: To avoid negative answers in the subtraction version, use a strip as shown below, with the digit 1 already written in the thousands place in the first number. The strategies now are interesting. Where would you try to put a card with a larger digit on it? Or a smaller one?

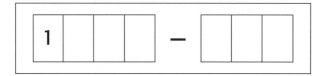

7.01: (a) The word 'sum' is incorrect; replace it with 'calculation'. (b) 'Adenoids' is incorrect; they are 'addends'. (c) The word 'minuet' is incorrect; it should be 'minuend'.

7.02: (a) These are not discrete sets, because some children are in both sets. One is a subset of the other. (b) On any given day these two sets are discrete; no child is in both sets. (c) These are not discrete sets; the letters *n*, *o* and *r* appear in both sets.

7.03: The union of the two sets contains 12 letters: *j, u, n, i, o, r, s, e, c, d, a, y*.

    For each of Questions 7.04–09 I provide below just one example of possible responses.

7.04: I need 250 ml of milk for one recipe and 125 ml of milk for another. How much milk is that altogether?

7.05: Ali is 15 years old. How old will he be in 40 years' time?

7.06: If it is 25 °C indoors and −6 °C outside, what is the difference in temperature?

7.07: A shirt costing £7.30 is reduced by £2.50. How much does it now cost?

7.08: The Australians scored 286 in a one-day cricket match. England has so far scored 196. How many more runs must they score to catch up with Australia?

7.09: So far this season, Arsenal has scored 24 goals and Chelsea 19. What is the difference in goals scored?

7.10: There are 35 years to wait. The calculation is 2061 − 2026. Inverse of addition.

7.11: Jill's pail is 1685 grams heavier. The calculation is 8135 − 6450. Comparison.

7.12: The butter left is 195 grams. The calculation is 250 − 55. Partitioning.

7.13: Start at 92 on the number line and count back 67.

7.14: Find the gap between 67 and 92 on the number line.

7.15: Start at 67 and add on until you get to 92.

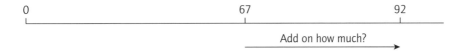

7.16: The calculation is 765 − 578 = 187. Inverse of addition.

7.17: The calculation is 32,457 − 14,589 = 17,868. Three sentences are: (a) 'The attendance at Manchester was 17,868 more than at Norwich.' (b) 'The attendance at Norwich was 17,868 less than at Manchester.' (c) 'The difference in attendance was 17,868.'

7.18: Key language: *spent*, *left*, *how much*. This might suggest subtraction, but actually it is an addition: 3.49 + 12.27. Answer £15.76.

7.19: Key language: *added to, altogether, how much*. This might suggest addition, but actually it is a subtraction: 127.25 – 13.40. Answer £113.85.

7.20: Key language: *takes, left, how many*. This might suggest subtraction, but actually it is an addition: 37 + 29. Answer 66.

7.21: Key language: *more than, how many*. This might suggest addition, but actually it is a subtraction: 349 – 137. Answer 212.

7.22: Key language: *weighs, less than*. This might suggest subtraction, but actually it is an addition: 27.8 + 4.7. Answer 32.5 kg.

7.23: Key language: *more than, more expensive than, how much*. This might suggest addition, but actually it is a subtraction: 365 – 128. Answer £237.

7.24: Key language: *more than, less than, difference*. This might suggest subtraction (comparison structure), but actually it is an addition: 128 + 365. Answer £493.

7.25: Here are some suggestions. Use the language 'I have 5 … and 3 more' for the addition. Show 5 fingers on one hand and put this behind your back; show the 3 with your other hand, asking how many altogether? 'So, I have 5 and 3 more, that's (counting on the fingers) 6, 7, 8.' Repeat with other small numbers. Show this on a line of numbered squares, as in many board games, with a counter on square 5; then throw a dice scoring, say, 3. Move on 3, counting out loud 6, 7, 8. Ask a 5-year-old how old they will be in 3 years' time: 'next birthday you will be 6, then 7, then 8' (matching the three numbers with three fingers).

7.26: Here are some suggestions:

- What is 8 plus 6?
- What is 14 minus 6?
- What is the sum of 6 and 8?
- What is the difference between 14 and 8?
- How old will an 8-year-old be in 6 years' time?
- How old will a 6-year-old be in 8 years' time?
- If the temperature is 14 degrees and it falls by 6 degrees, what is it now?
- The temperature last night was 8 degrees. It has now increased by 6 degrees. What is the temperature now?
- The pencil costs 6p and the ball-point pen costs 14p. How much cheaper is the pencil?
- Which is the greater: 8 add 6, or 6 add 8?
- (To the children) Now, who can make up their own question about 6, 8 and 14?

7.27: A correct interpretation. Aggregation structure (how many altogether).

7.28: A correct interpretation. Augmentation structure (increasing in volume).

7.29: A correct interpretation. Aggregation structure (how many altogether).

7.30: Not a correct story, unless the child means 'how many did they have altogether?'

7.31: A correct interpretation. Aggregation structure (how many altogether).

7.32: A correct interpretation. Augmentation structure (increasing in price).

7.33: A correct interpretation. Augmentation structure (increasing in height).

7.34: A correct interpretation. Partitioning structure (how many left).

7.35: A correct interpretation. Partitioning structure (how many kilograms left).

7.36: A correct interpretation. Comparison (how much older).

7.37: A correct interpretation. Partitioning (how many are not).

7.38: A correct interpretation. Reduction (in price).

7.39: This is not a correct story for 28 – 16.

7.40: A correct interpretation. Inverse of addition (how many years must be added).

7.41: Doing additions by 'counting on' (see Question 7.25) uses the augmentation structure. So, for example, 7 + 5 is interpreted as '7 count on 5'. A common mistake, particularly when using fingers, is to start counting at the 7, so getting to 11 rather than 12. It helps pupils to learn to say '7, and 5 more', which makes clearer the augmentation structure and the notion that the 7 is not part of the 'five more'.

7.42: Doing subtractions on a number line by counting back uses the reduction structure. So, for example, 15 – 6 is interpreted as '15 count back 6'. The child may be making the following error here. Counting back 6 steps from 15 gets you to 9. But because the language of 'take away' is so strongly attached to subtraction, the child thinks they have taken away the 9, so the answer is 8. The language 'take away' is inappropriate for this procedure. Encourage the child to talk about counting back so many steps, to see where they get to: emphasize that we are counting the steps, not the points on the number line.

7.43: Two bars are used, as shown below. The top bar represents the number of stamps that Suzy has. Write 349 in this bar. The bar underneath represents Gill's stamps; number unknown, so put a question mark in this bar. Add another bar to the right of Gill's to make the second row of the diagram as long as the first. Write 137, the number of stamps more than Gill that Suzy has, in this bar. The bar with the question mark is, of course, the answer to the question. The bar model shows that the calculation required is 349 – 137.

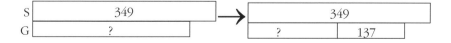

7.44: Two bars are used, as shown below. The top bar represents the weight in kg of Gill's case (not yet known, but the answer to the question) and the lower bar that of Suzy (27.8 kg, so write this in the bar.) Because the weight of Gill's case is greater than Suzy's, the upper bar must extend beyond the lower bar. This extension represents the 4.7 kg difference. Show this on the bar-model. It should be clear now that the weight of Gill's case in kg is 27.8 + 4.7.

S	?		→		?	
G	27.8				27.8	4.7

8.01: True for all values of p.

8.02: True for all values of p.

8.03: This statement is not true for any values of p. Try $p = 10$, for example. Left of the equals sign is 25 – 2 (which is 23), and right of the equals sign is 15 – 8 (which is 7).

8.04: True for all values of p.

8.05: This statement is not true for any values of p. For example, try $p = 10$. Left of the equals sign is 25 – 18 (which is 7), and right of the equals sign is 15 + 8 (which is 23).

8.06: commutative

8.07: associative

8.08: multiples

8.09: hundred, empty

8.10: 386 + 243 = (300 + 80 + 6) + (200 + 40 + 3). Adding the hundreds, then the tens, then the units, this becomes 500 + 120 + 9 = 620 + 9 = 629.

8.11: 247 + 245 is nearly double 245 (= 490). Compensating by adding on the extra 2, we get 247 + 245 = 492.

8.12: Double 144 is 288, so 288 – 144 = 144. Compensating for the additional 1, we get 287 – 144 = 143.

8.13: A friendlier calculation is 729 – 629. That gives the answer 100. But 734 is 5 more than 729, so we add another 5 to the answer, to get 734 – 629 = 105.

8.14: Subtract 200 and then compensate by adding 2 to the answer. 513 – 200 = 313. So 513 – 198 = 315.

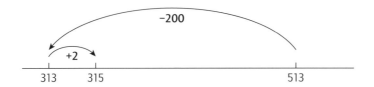

8.15: Move from 678 to 680 (adding 2) to 700 (adding 20) to 900 (adding 200) to 924 (adding 24), giving 924 − 678 = 2 + 20 + 200 + 24 = 246.

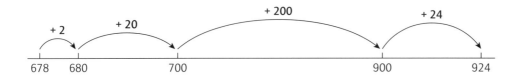

8.16: Counting on 2 from 1098 gets us to 1100; counting on a further 4 gets to 1004.

8.17: Remarkably, they are anagrams.

8.18: 892 − 566 = 892 − (600 − 34) = 892 − 600 + 34

8.19: 892 − 566 = 892 − (500 + 66) = 892 − 500 − 66

8.20: 892 − 566 = (900 − 8) − (600 − 34) = 900 − 600 + 34 − 8

8.21: 892 − 566 = (900 − 8) − (500 + 66) = 900 − 500 − 66 − 8

8.22: £1486. One way is to add on from 5879, using 5880, 5900, 6000 and 7000 as stepping stones, giving 1 + 20 + 100 + 1000 + 365 = 1486.

8.23: The total cost is £873. One way is to start with 500 + 377 (877), then compensate by subtracting 4 to get 496 + 377 = 873. The total cost is £127 short of the budget. Calculate this by adding on from 873 to 1000, using 880 and 900 as stepping stones: so 1000 − 873 = 7 + 20 + 100 = 127.

8.24: You should find that the result is always 1089. The explanation for this involves some tricky algebra. You can find it on the internet by searching for '1089 trick'. There's even a book called *1089 and All That: A Journey into Mathematics*, by David Acheson (OUP, 2010).

8.25: The eight numbers you can reach are: 34, 36, 43, 47, 63, 67, 74, 76.

8:26: These moves correspond to: − 21, − 19, − 12, − 8, + 8, + 12, + 19, + 21.

8.27: If you are at 34 after one move, for example, and make a move of + 12, you get to 46. One way to tackle this problem is to compile a table showing all such possible combinations of a starting point after one move (34, 36, 43 and so on) and the next move (– 21, – 19, – 12 and so on), as follows:

	– 21	– 19	– 12	– 8	+ 8	+ 12	+ 19	+ 21
34	13	15	22	26	42	46	53	55
36	15	17	24	28	44	48	55	57
43	22	24	31	35	51	55	62	64
47	26	28	35	39	55	59	66	68
63	42	44	51	55	71	75	82	84
67	46	48	55	59	75	79	86	88
74	53	55	62	66	82	86	93	95
76	55	57	64	68	84	88	95	97

So there are actually 33 possible squares to finish on after two knight's moves starting from 55: 13, 15, 17, 22, 24, 26, 28, 31, 35, 39, 42, 44, 46, 48, 51, 53, 55, 57, 59, 62, 64, 66, 68, 71, 75, 79, 82, 84, 86, 88, 93, 95, 97. This illustrates why chess is such a challenging game. Notice that most of these can be reached by more than one combination.

8.28: These pairs of moves correspond to adding or subtracting 42, 40, 38, 33, 31, 29, 27, 24, 20, 16, 13, 9, 7, 4, 2 and 0.

8.29: See diagram below. The children put 8 counters in one frame and 6 in the other, as shown. This helps them to see 8 as 5 and 3, and 6 as 5 add 1. Then (a) leaving the counters as they are they could mentally add the two 5s to make 10, and the 3 and 1 to make 4. (b) They could move 2 of the 6 counters in the second frame to fill the first frame, leaving 4 in the second frame. In each case they see the total to be 10 + 4, which hopefully they will recognize as 14.

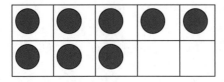 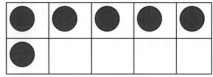

8.30: Here are two suggestions; see diagrams below. (a) Using 'take away' they put out 13 counters, 10 in one ten-frame and 3 in the other; they then remove 8 counters, 3 from the second frame and 5 from the first, to give the result as 5. (b) Using 'what must be added?' they put out 8 counters in the first frame, then find how many more counters they need to increase this to 13 counters: 2 in the first frame and 3 in the next.

(a)

(b)

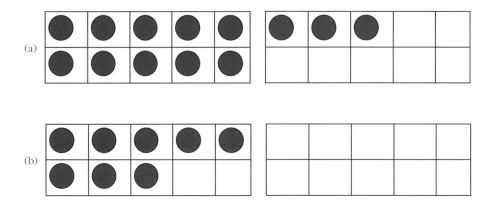

8.31: $1000 - 236 = 764$.

8.32: It is likely that the child gets 800 by subtracting 200 from 1000, the 70 by subtracting 30 from 100 and the 4 by subtracting 6 from 10.

8.33: Start by asking the child to add the 874 back on to the 236, to reveal that the answer is incorrect. To identify the error, ask the child to calculate $80 - 26$. Show this on a number line as adding on from 26. Look at the first digit in the answer (54) and note that it is not just $8 - 2$. Why not? Try some other examples to reinforce this point: $50 - 17$ is not forty-something; $93 - 39$ is not sixty-something and so on. The child should now be able to tackle $1000 - 236$ and similar examples, using adding on and a number line.

8.34: You might use this to demonstrate adding 21 by partitioning it into $20 + 1$. Start at 37 on the hundred square, count on 2 tens and 1 unit, by moving down 2 rows and forward 1 square.

8.35: Partition the 43 into 4 tens and 3 units. Start at the 96, count back 4 tens and 3 units, by moving up 4 rows and back 3 squares.

8.36: You might use this to demonstrate the advantage of starting with the larger number in an addition, i.e. change it to $57 + 8$. Then show how 'add 8' can usefully be split up into 'add 3' (to get to 60) and then 'add 5'.

8.37: Split the 'add 16' into 'add 10' (to get to 47), then 'add 3' (to get to 50), then 'add 3' again.

8.38: Think of $43 - 17$ as finding the gap between 17 and 43 on the hundred square. Do this in various ways, counting on from 17. For example, add 20, then 3, then 3 again ($20 + 3 + 3 = 26$). Or add 30 (to get to 47), count back 4, so the answer is $30 - 4 = 26$.

8.39: You might add the 19 by adding 20 (move down 2 rows), then moving back 1 square, demonstrating compensation.

8.40: Subtract the 19 by counting back 20 (move up two rows), then moving forward 1 square, because you have gone too far back – again demonstrating compensation.

8.41: The child has just added the two numbers in each position (hundreds, tens and ones), not understanding that the 13 tens have to be exchanged for 1 hundred and 3 tens. A good starting point for helping the child would be to ask them to calculate 300 + 142 mentally and to note that the answer is nothing like 3138. Then ask them how to compensate for the additional 4.

8.42: The child has just found the difference between the two digits in each position, thus avoiding the problem of how to deal with 7 – 8 in the tens position. A good starting point would be to ask the child how we might make the second number more friendly. This could lead to changing it to 175 (375 – 175 = 200). Then, ask how much more we are subtracting if we subtract 184 rather than 175.

8.43: The child appears to have ignored the 0 in the tens position for 703 and just written down the 8. Children often do this because they think of zero as being 'nothing'. So, 'nothing' is being done to the 8. Perhaps ask the child to think about adding on from 482 to get to 703, using 490, 500 and 700 as stepping stones.

8.44: This is probably an error caused by using compensation but compensating in the wrong direction. So the child subtracts 240 (to get 333) and then subtracts another 1, rather than adding it. Ask the child whether they have to take away more or less than 240 (less). If you take away less, is the result larger or smaller? Demonstrate with smaller numbers, using a pile of counters or something visual.

8.45: In pan A put 3 hundred-gram and 6 one-gram masses (306 grams). In pan B put 1 hundred-gram, 2 ten-gram and 4 one-gram masses (124 grams). Then balance the two by adding masses to pan B: this will require 1 hundred-gram mass (note that 2 of these is too much), then 8 ten-gram masses and 2 one-gram masses. So the original pan A was 182 grams heavier than pan B; pan B was 182 grams lighter than pan A; hence the difference between 306 and 124 is 182.

9.01: The missing numbers, in order from left to right, are: (second line) 600, 10; (third line) 1100, 80, 11, 8191.

9.02: The missing numbers are: 7000; 1100; 10, 80; 2, 9, 11; 8191.

9.03: The missing number is 8191.

9.04: The missing numbers, in order from left to right, are: (top line) 5000, 60; (third line) 600, 10; (bottom line) 900, 50, 3, 4953.

9.05: The missing numbers are 5 (above the 6 thousand) and 4953 (the answer).

9.06: 8274 − 1496 = 8278 − 1500 (adding 4 to both numbers)

   = 8778 − 2000 (adding 500 to both numbers)

   = 6778

9.07: 7021 − 2893 = 7028 − 2900 (adding 7 to both numbers)

   = 7128 − 3000 (adding 100 to both numbers)

   = 4128

9.08: The calculation is set out with 703 in the top line and 498 underneath it. One of the hundreds in the 703 then has to be exchanged for 10 tens, and one of these tens for 10 ones. The top number is now decomposed into 6 hundreds, 9 tens and 13 ones. The subtraction of 4 hundreds, 9 tens and 8 ones can then be done easily, to give the answer 205. Check that 205 + 498 = 703.

9.09: The calculation is set out with 4006 in the top line and 278 underneath it, making sure the 8 is written directly underneath the 6 (in the units position). One of the thousands in the 4006 then has to be exchanged for 10 hundreds, then one of these tens for 10 tens, and then one of these for 10 ones. The top number is now decomposed into 3 thousands, 9 hundreds, 9 tens and 16 ones. The subtraction of 2 hundreds, 7 tens and 8 ones can then be done easily, to give the answer 3728. Check that 3728 + 278 = 4006.

9.10: The problem here is in subtracting the 4 tens in 12,345, when there are no tens in the number above. One of the 2 ten-thousands in 20,005 is exchanged for 10 thousands, one of these is then exchanged for 10 hundreds, and then one of these is exchanged for 10 tens. The top number is now decomposed into 1 ten thousand, 9 thousands, 9 hundreds, 10 tens and 5 ones. The subtraction of 1 ten thousand, 2 thousands, 3 hundreds, 4 tens and 5 ones can now be done easily, to give the answer 7660. Check that 7660 + 12,345 = 20,005.

9.11: A = 9, B = 1, C = 5, D = 8, E = 3, F = 0.

9.12: £1486. To check: 5879 + 1486 = 7365.

9.13: Total cost = £873. This is £127 short of the total budget.

9.14: I hope you decided that you prefer the informal methods.

9.15: The total attendance is 59,114.

9.16: The difference is 3402.

9.17: For calculations with five-digit numbers, a formal written algorithm is often preferable (but not as efficient as using a calculator).

9.18: The error is in adding the hundreds (1 + 9 = 10) and writing down the 10, not 'carrying the one' into the thousands column. The correct answer is 10,042.

9.19: The error is not lining up the units, tens and hundreds, from the right, so the addition done is actually 4028 + 6280. The correct answer for 4028 + 628 is 4656.

9.20: The error is subtracting the smaller digit from the larger one in each column, thus avoiding the need for any decomposition. The correct answer is 745.

9.21: The error is that the ten added to the units column to make 3 into 13 is not obtained from the tens column. The 6 tens in the top number should be reduced to 5, to complete the process of decomposition. The correct answer is 3107.

9.22: A possible series of questions might be:

- How do we say this first number (pointing to the numeral 53)?
- How can we show this number using these tens and unit blocks? (Set out the blocks.)
- How do we say the number we have to add to this (pointing to 37)?
- How can we show this number using these tens and units blocks? (Set out the blocks.)
- Now, how many unit blocks do we have? (Ten)
- What can we exchange these for? (Another ten blocks. Do the exchange.)
- Now we have five tens here, three here and the one we have made from ten units. How many tens altogether? (Nine.)
- So, altogether, when we have added the two numbers, we have how many tens? How many units? (Nine, none.)
- So, the answer to the addition is …? (ninety)

9.23: A possible series of questions might be:

- How do we say this number (pointing to the numeral 72)?
- How can we show this number using these tens and units blocks? (Set out the blocks.)
- How many tens and units do we have to subtract from the 72? (Point to the 48, 4 tens and 8 units.)
- Do we have enough units to take away eight units?
- What can we exchange to get some more units? (One of the tens. Do the exchange, making 6 tens and 12 units.)
- Now can we subtract 8 units? (Do this, leaving 6 tens and 4 units.)
- So, all that's left to do now is to subtract the 4 tens …

9.24: A possible series of questions might be:

- How do we say this first number (pointing to 469)?
- How can we show this number using these hundreds, tens and units blocks? (Set out the blocks.)
- How do we say the number we have to add to this (pointing to 372)?
- How can we show this number using these hundreds, tens and units blocks? (Set out the blocks.)
- Now, how many unit blocks are there altogether? (Eleven.)
- Can we exchange some of these for a ten block? (Do the exchange, leaving one unit.)
- Now we have six tens here, seven here and the one we have carried. How many tens is that altogether?
- Can we exchange some of these tens for a hundred block? (Do the exchange, leaving four tens.)
- Now we have four hundreds here, three here and the one we have carried. How many hundreds is that altogether? (Eight.)
- So, altogether, when we have added the two numbers, we have how many hundreds? How many tens? How many units? (Eight, four, one.)
- So, the answer to the addition is …? (841)

9.25: A possible series of questions might be:

- How do we say this number (pointing to 628)?
- How can we show this number using these hundreds, tens and units blocks? (Set out the blocks.)
- How many hundreds, tens and units do we have to subtract from the 628? (Point to the 473.)
- Let's start by taking away the three units. How many units are left? (Five.)
- Now, how many tens do we have to subtract? (Point to the 473: seven tens.)
- Do we have enough tens to take away seven of them?
- How can we get some more tens? What can we exchange for tens? (One of the hundreds.)
- One hundred can be exchanged for how many tens? (Do the exchange, leaving five hundreds and making 12 tens.)
- Now take away the seven tens. How many tens are left? (Five.)
- Now, how many hundreds do we have to subtract? (Point to the 473: four hundreds.)
- So, we take away four hundreds. How many are left? (One.)

- So, after we have done the subtraction, we are left with how many hundreds? How many tens? How many units? (One, five, five.)
- So the answer to the subtraction is ...? (155)

9.26: It's not easy to express these clearly in words, without being able to point at digits and columns, but here are some possible key principles:

- Always lay out the two numbers carefully in columns for hundreds, tens and units, with plenty of space in between.
- Work along the columns from right to left, starting with the units.
- In each column, always subtract the bottom number from the top number.
- If the top number in your column is smaller than the bottom number, then exchange one in the next column for ten in your column.
- If you cannot do this because there is a zero in that column, then go to the next column that has a non-zero number in it, exchange one of these for ten in the column to the right, and work your way back, always exchanging 'one of these for ten of those'.
- Check your answer by doing an addition.

10.01: The 7 is the *multiplier* and the 35 is the *product*.

10.02: The *ratio* of 75 to 25 is 3.

10.03: The word *per* means 'for each'.

10.04: It has been *scaled* by a *factor* of 2.

10.05: 28 divided by 3 is 9, with a *remainder* of 1.

10.06: The four statements are $3 \times 8 = 24$, $8 \times 3 = 24$, $24 \div 8 = 3$ and $24 \div 3 = 8$.

10.07: Commutativity: $3 \times 8 = 8 \times 3$; 3 rows of eight is the same as 8 rows of three.

10.08: Some examples of stories are:

- I bought 6 pens costing 15p each. How much altogether? (6 lots of 15, in the context of shopping.)
- Jon earns £6 per hour. How much does he earn in 15 hours? (15 lots of 6, in the contexts of money and time, using 'per'.)
- A scale drawing of the classroom uses a scale of 1 to 15. On the scale drawing, a desk is 6 cm wide. How wide is it in reality? (Scaling by a factor of 15.)

10.09: Some examples of stories are:

- How many weeks will it take me to save 60 tokens, if I save 12 each week? (Inverse of multiplication, repeated addition to reach a target.)
- 60 litres of water is to be shared equally between 12 buckets. How much in each bucket? (Sharing equally between, in the context of liquid volume.)

- How many times faster is a car going at 60 mph than a cyclist going at 12 mph? (Ratio.)

10.10: $\frac{1}{3}$ (one-third)

10.11: When a is less than b (and a is not 0, because division by zero is not possible).

10.12: When a is greater than b.

10.13: When $a = 0$ (and b is not 0).

10.14: $b \div a$ is not possible, because a is 0 and you cannot divide by zero.

10.15: When $a = b$ (provided they are not zero).

10.16: The division by zero in line 3 is not allowed.

10.17: A's hourly rate is 3 times greater than B's hourly rate.

10.18: The ratio is 3.

10.19: It stays the same. For example, double both rates: A = £120, B = £40; the ratio is still 3.

10.20: It stays the same. For example, halve both rates: A = £30, B = £10; the ratio is still 3.

10.21: It decreases. For example, increase both by £20: A = £80, B = £40; the ratio is now 2.

10.22: It increases. For example, decrease both by £10: A = £50, B = £10; the ratio is now 5.

10.23: £5 and £12.50 cannot be their pocket money because they are not multiples of £1.50.

10.24: Jo actually gets more toys. We might be surprised, because one toy at 50p and one at £1 would cost the same as two toys at 75p, so we think surely they get the same number of toys. But, take an example: assume they get £6 a month for pocket money. Jo gets 12 toys one month and 6 the next, making 18 in total. But Jack gets 8 toys each month, which makes a total of 16 toys.

10.25: What's the cost of 9 envelopes at 6p each? (Answer: 54p)

10.26: How many envelopes costing 6p each can I buy for 54p? (Answer: 9)

10.27: Jack is 9 years old, his granny is 54. How many times older is his granny than Jack? (Answer: she is 6 times older.)

10.28: Some examples of questions are:

- How many nines make 54?
- How many sixes make 54?

- What's 54 divided by 9?
- What's 54 divided by 6?
- How many boxes of six eggs contain 54 eggs altogether?
- If I cycle at 9 mph, how far will I go in 6 hours?
- How many boxes do I need to hold 54 books, at 9 in a box?
- Share 54p between 6 people. How much is that each?
- I spend £6 a week on newspapers. How many weeks does it take me to spend £54?
- How many rows of 9 chairs are needed to seat 54 people?

10.29: Here are some ideas. Aim to bring out the same mathematics of a rectangular array as in Questions 10.06 and 10.07. Ask questions that make it clear that 5 rows of 6 pots and 6 rows of 5 pots are the same. Use the language '5 sets of 6 equals 6 sets of 5'. Look at the arrangement as division in terms of equal sharing between: '30 pots in 5 rows, how many in each row?' and '30 pots in 6 rows, how many in each row?' Also, look at division as the inverse of multiplication: 'How many rows of 5? How many rows of 6?' Count the pots in 5s a row at a time; and likewise in 6s.

10.30: Show, for example, that, starting at zero, 3 steps of 4 gets you to the same place as 4 steps of 3. Use a number of different examples. It's useful to do this with two children side by side taking steps along a paved path.

10.31: Ask children what a step of zero would mean. Take 25 steps of zero along a number line, starting at zero, and where do you get to? You do not move. Also, for example, if 3×5 means 3 steps of 5, 2×5 means 2 steps of 5, and 1×5 means 1 step of 5, what does 0×5 mean? Where does it get you to? Again, this can be done with children on a paved pathway being instructed to take no steps forward five times. Or, to take five steps forward no times.

10.32: Ask questions like: how many steps of 4 do you need to get from zero to 20? This is $20 \div 4$, using the inverse of multiplication.

10.33: We would need to find how many steps of zero get us from zero to 20. But with steps of zero you're going nowhere.

11.01: Uncle Bob has £24 to share between his 2 nephews. How much do they each get?

11.02: Uncle Bob has £24 to share between his 12 nieces. How much do they each get?

11.03: $23 \times 19 = 23 \times (20 - 1) = (23 \times 20) - (23 \times 1) = 460 - 23 = 437$.

11.04: $41 \times 1 = 41$, $41 \times 2 = 82$, $41 \times 4 = 164$, $41 \times 8 = 328$, $41 \times 16 = 656$. Since $23 = 1 + 2 + 4 + 16$, then $41 \times 23 = 41 + 82 + 164 + 656 = 943$.

11.05: Subtract 10 lots of 24 (240) from 408, leaving 168. Subtract 5 lots of 24 (120) from this, leaving 48. This is 2 lots of 24. So $408 \div 24 = 10 + 5 + 2 = 17$.

11.06: $408 \div 24 = 204 \div 12 = 102 \div 6 = 51 \div 3 = 17$.

11.07: $319 \div 11 = (99 + 220) \div 11 = 9 + 20 = 29$.

11.08: The distributive law for multiplication distributed across subtraction (after replacing the 18 by $20 - 2$).

11.09: The associate law for multiplication (after replacing the 48 by 4×12).

11.10: The distributive law for division distributed across addition (after replacing the 168 by $160 + 8$).

11.11: $84 \times 56 = 4704$ (using the commutative property).

11.12: $560 \times 84 = 47{,}040$ (multiplying by 10).

11.13: Below are seven of the numerous possibilities:

(a) $84 \times 57 = 4788$ (adding another 84)

(b) $840 \times 56 = 47{,}040$ (multiplying by 10)

(c) $840 \times 5600 = 4{,}704{,}000$ (multiplying by 10 and by 100)

(d) $84 \times 5.6 = 470.4$ (dividing 56 by 10)

(e) $42 \times 56 = 2352$ (halving the 84)

(f) $84 \times 28 = 2352$ (halving the 56)

(g) $85 \times 56 = 4760$ (adding another 56)

11.14: Below are four of the numerous possibilities:

(a) $4704 \div 84 = 56$ (division, the inverse of multiplication)

(b) $4704 \div 56 = 84$ (division, the inverse of multiplication)

(c) $2352 \div 56 = 42$ (division as inverse of multiplication result in 11.13(e))

(d) $4760 \div 56 = 85$ (division as inverse of multiplication result in 11.13(g))

11.15: 99, 399, 899, 1599 and 2499

11.16: Choose a number that is a multiple of 10. Multiply 1 less than the number by 1 more than it. The answer is 1 less than the number multiplied by itself. [This is actually true of *any* number. See Question 11.17, for example.]

11.17: 199×201 will be $200 \times 200 - 1 = 39{,}999$

11.18: 1368 (1 less than 37×37)

11.19: Each of the 24 bees has 6 legs so that's 144 legs altogether. The challenge of this jigsaw is definitely the bees' knees.

11.20: You need 8 coaches. Mrs Haylock did this question in ten seconds; but she was a regular watcher of *Countdown*, so she knew her 75-times table. Just use doubling … 2 coaches seat 150, 4 coaches seat 300, 8 coaches seat 600.

11.21: £126. Derek set this question for Ralph and he did it in less than 30 seconds without writing anything down. It helps if you use factors to think of 24 × 25 as 6 × 100. The total of monthly payments is £600 + £6 = £606.

11.22: First, ask the children to work out mentally 75 × 2. Then ask how we can use this result to work out 75 × 4 (by doubling it). And from this, 75 × 12 (by multiplying by 3).

11.23: Ask for 75 × 2 and 75 × 10, the calculations to be done mentally. Write these on the board. Ask how we could use these to get 75 × 12 (by adding them). Ask a child to explain why (we have two 75s and ten 75s, so if we add them we have twelve 75s).

11.24: Write in a column on the board, 1 × 12, 2 × 12, 4 × 12, 8 × 12, 16 × 12, 32 × 12, 64 × 12, and get the children to supply the answers using doubling. Ask questions like, how many 12s would we have if we added the first three results? The last two? The first and the last? Which of these should we add to get 75 lots of 12?

11.25: What is 100 × 12? So what is 50 × 12? (Halve it.) And what is 25 × 12? (Halve it again.) How could we use what we have here to find 75 × 12?

11.26: Look at the rectangular array of tiles as 10 rows of 37 (370) and 3 rows of 37. Then ask how to deal with 3 × 37. The children may suggest breaking this down into 3 rows of 30 (90) and 3 rows of 7 (21). This gives a total of 370 + 90 + 21 = 481 tiles.

11.27: The common error is to think that by adding 1 to one of the numbers in a product you add 1 to the answer, without thinking about what the mathematical symbols mean. To help the children to answer this question, ask what they would add to the array of 13 rows of 37 tiles to make it 13 rows of 38 tiles. Use a picture to demonstrate that they have to add another 13 tiles.

11.28: Partition the 15 boxes into 10 boxes in one set and 5 boxes in another set. Ask the children to calculate how many pencils there are in each set (10 × 12 and 5 × 12). So, how many altogether? (120 + 60 = 180).

11.29: Ask a child to put the 15 boxes into three equal sets. Remind them that there are 12 in each box. How many pencils are there in each of the three sets? (5 × 12 = 60). So, how many altogether? (60 × 3 = 180).

11.30: Ask the children to work out how many blue pencils there are. This calculation, 15×6, can be done by thinking of it as 10 sixes add 5 sixes ($60 + 30 = 90$). So, how many red? And how many altogether? ($90 + 90 = 180$).

11.31: Take 2 pencils out of each of the boxes and place them on the table. Ask how many pencils are left in each box (10) and how many altogether in the boxes ($15 \times 10 = 150$). Ask how many pencils are on the table ($15 \times 2 = 30$). So, how many pencils in total? ($150 + 30 = 180$).

11.32: 7 subtract 3 gives 4. This 4 multiplied by 25 is 100.

11.33: 7 multiplied by 8 is 56 and $9 - 6 = 3$. Then $56 + 3 = 59$.

11.34: 63 divided by 7 is 9 and $13 - 8 = 5$. Then 9 multiplied by 5 gives 45.

11.35: One solution is $75 + 1 = 76$. Then multiply 76 by 7 to get 532. Add 9 and add 2 to get 543.

11.36: The other result with this pattern is $56 = 7 \times 8$, which many children (and adults) find difficult to remember. Just chanting 'five, six, seven eight; 56 is seven eights' can help some to remember this product. Incidentally, there is no deep mathematical explanation as to why this works; it just does.

11.37: There are 12 non-fiction books (and 48 fiction books).

11.38: N stands for the number of non-fiction books and F for the number of fiction books. See the bar-modelling diagram below. Underneath a bar representing the total of 60 books, we have a small box representing N and a larger one representing F. How many Ns would be needed to replace the F? Remember F is four times N. So, the whole of the second bar can be replaced by 5 Ns, as shown. Hence N is 60 divided by 5.

12.01: The calculation is: $139 \times 20 = 2780$.

12.02: The calculation is: $139 \times 4 = 556$.

12.03: The calculation is $2780 + 556 = 3336$.

12.04: The calculations are: $100 \times 20 = 2000$; $30 \times 20 = 600$; $9 \times 20 = 180$; $100 \times 4 = 400$.

12.05: The calculations are: $30 \times 4 = 120$; $9 \times 4 = 36$; $2000 + 600 + 180 + 400 + 120 + 36 = 3336$.

12.06: See the diagram overleaf.

	100	30	9
20	100 × 20	30 × 20	9 × 20
4	100 × 4	30 × 4	9 × 4

12.07: The 2 and the 5 together represent 250 or 25 tens. When these are divided by 7, you get 3 tens in the quotient, and 4 tens remaining. The little 4 represents these 4 remaining tens, that is, 40.

12.08: From the top, the missing numbers are 198 (478 − 280), 5 (because 5 lots of 28 make 140), 58 (198 − 140), 17 (the sum of 10, 5 and 2) and 2 (58 − 56).

12.09: The missing numbers are 28, 168 and 10.

12.10: The dividend (the number being divided) is 2086 and the divisor is 42. Note that the 4 in the answer and the 168 in the calculation imply that the divisor multiplied by 4 equals 168.

12.11: A = 0, B = 4, C = 8, D = 1.

12.12: P = 9, Q = 8.

12.13: You need to calculate (23 × 35) × 17 or (17 × 23) × 35 or (17 × 35) × 23. The answer is £13,685.

12.14: You need to calculate 778 ÷ 23. The answer to this division is 33, remainder 19. So, to meet the target 34 teachers are required.

12.15: You need to calculate 500 ÷ 36. This gives the answer 13, remainder 32. So, 13 trays can be filled. The farmer is 4 eggs short of filling another tray.

12:16: 74 × 3 = (70 × 3) + (4 × 3) = 210 + 12 = 222.

12.17: 74 × 6 = 444; 74 × 9 = 666; 74 × 12 = 888.

12.18: 74 × 15 = (74 × 9) + (74 × 6) = 666 + 444 = 1110.

12.19: 74 × 39 = (74 × 15) + (74 × 15) + (74 × 9) = 1110 + 1110 + 666 = 2886.

12.20: You could split the 63 into 15 + 15 + 15 + 15 + 3. So, 74 × 63 = 1110 + 1110 + 1110 + 1110 + 222 = 4662.

12.21: Here is the calculation done by long multiplication:

$$
\begin{array}{r}
74 \\
\times \quad 63 \\
\hline
4440 \\
222 \\
\hline
4662 \\
\end{array}
$$

12.22: Ask the children how to partition 12 and 15 into tens and ones (10 + 2 and 10 + 5). Show how the 12 rows can be separated into 10 rows and 2 rows. Ask what we can do like this with the 15 columns. Draw two lines to show these partitions. Ask a child to point to the four sections produced. Now get the children to say how many squares there are in each section. Look for language like '10 rows of 10 squares', '10 rows of 5 squares', '2 rows of 10 squares' and '2 rows of 5 squares'. Record the four results on the board and ask the children to find the total number of squares.

12.23: Some points to make in a response to this complaint: (a) there is no 'proper' method for doing multiplication; (b) different cultures use a variety of methods; (c) the grid method is actually the same process as long multiplication, but it is just slightly less compact, using, for example, four internal multiplications instead of two; (d) so, when finding, say, 67×48, instead of finding 67×8 in one go, it does it in two steps, 60×8 and 7×8; (e) it is easier to understand and in line with an approach to teaching mathematics based on understanding rather than on rote learning; (f) we will teach them long multiplication in due course, but they will progress to that with greater confidence if they have understood this method first; (g) but, actually, in real life, with the availability of calculators, no one needs to do multiplications more difficult than those that can be done easily and efficiently by the grid method.

12.24: Here are some key points that would go on my list (using 47×36 as an example):

- Learners have first to be fluent and accurate in their recall of multiplication facts up to 10×10. [In the example, they would need to recall 7×3, 4×3, 7×6 and 4×6.]
- Learners have to be fluent and accurate in the standard column method for addition. [In the example, they will need to add 1410 and 282.]
- Set out the calculation with plenty of space and be careful to line up the hundreds, tens and units in columns.
- Learners have to be able to multiply a two-digit number by a single-digit number, preferably doing the carrying in their head. [For example, for 47×36 they have to be able to calculate 47×3 and 47×6.]
- If they need to write down the numbers being carried, suggest that they do it somewhere else on the paper rather than in the middle of the long multiplication. Then cross it out when they have carried it. [In my example, when finding 47×6 they start with $7 \times 6 = 42$, write down the 2 in the units column and have to remember to carry the 4 into the tens.]
- Have a policy as to whether to start by multiplying by the tens [the 30 in 36] or by the units [the 6 in 36] and stick to this.

- Help learners to understand why, for example, multiplying by 30 can be done by writing a zero in the units column and then multiplying by 3.
- Discuss with learners when long multiplication might be an appropriate method to use. For example, 47 × 36, yes; 20 × 12, no.

12.25: The error is in multiplying 63 by 7 and getting 4221. The child is forgetting that the 2 in the 21 represents 2 tens that have to be carried over to the tens column and added to the result of multiplying 6 tens by 7. This is a common difficulty in long multiplication. It is avoided by use of the grid or area method, where 60 × 7 and 3 × 7 would be done as two separate steps.

12.26: The error here is 20 × 0 = 20. This is also a common mistake, probably associated with thinking of zero as 'nothing': if you multiply 20 by 'nothing' then you still have the 20. The second line of the multiplication is completely superfluous, since the first line gives the result for 20 × 10. I would be really disappointed to see a child using long multiplication for this calculation.

12.27: The 2 × 50 and 2 × 2 should be 20 × 50 and 20 × 2. The child has not used the fact that the 2 in 24 represents 20. Again, this is an error that is unlikely to occur when using the grid or area method, in which the 24 is partitioned into 20 and 4.

12.28: The error is in the subtraction of 75 from 80 to give (wrongly) 15. Being efficient in subtraction is a prerequisite for doing long division. Long division is not the most efficient way of doing this calculation anyway. It is much easier to use the fact that there are four 25s in 100, hence 32 in 800.

13.01: See the diagram below:

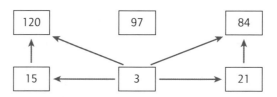

13.02: See the diagram below:

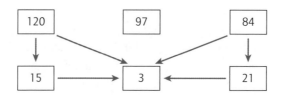

13.03: All the arrows in Question 13.01 are reversed in Question 13.02, and vice versa. This is because 'multiple of' and 'factor of' are inverse relationships. In each diagram, there are groups of three numbers connected by triangles of arrows, illustrating transitivity: 3, 15 and 120; and 3, 21 and 84.

13.04: False. It would be true to say that 17 is a factor of 68, or 68 is a multiple of 17.

13.05: True. 1 is a factor of every natural number.

13.06: True. See the solutions to Questions 13.01 and 13.02 above.

13.07: False. It may be true sometimes, but it is not true in general. For example, the digital root of 26 is 8; double this to get 52, which has a digital root of 7.

13.08: True. $1 + 2 + 3 + 4 + 5 + 6 + 7 + 8 + 9 = 45$, then $4 + 5 = 9$.

13.09: True. Any number with a digital root of 9 is a multiple of 9.

13.10: True. Because 3 is a factor of 12.

13.11: False. The lowest common multiple of 6 and 12 is 12.

13.12: True. Note that 91 is not prime (7 and 13 are factors).

13.13: False. There is an even prime number, namely 2.

13.14: A multiple of 7 is a positive whole number (or 'a natural number') that can be divided *exactly* by 7 (or 'without a remainder').

13.15: A factor of 280 is a positive whole number that 280 can be divided by exactly, without a remainder.

13.16: A prime number is a natural number that has exactly two factors (1 and itself).

13.17: A rectangular or composite number is a natural number that can be represented by more than one row of counters, with the same number in each row.

13.18: 121 is the square number ($= 11^2$).

13.19: 125 is the cube number ($= 5^3$).

13.20: 136 is the triangle number ($= 1 + 2 + 3 + 4 + 5 + 6 + 7 + 8 + 9 + 10 + 11 + 12 + 13 + 14 + 15 + 16$). 120 is also a triangle number, but strictly it is not *between* 120 and 140.

13.21: Two possible answers are 130 ($2 \times 5 \times 13$) and 138 ($2 \times 3 \times 23$).

13.22: $10 > \sqrt{50}$ (because 10^2 is 100, which is greater than 50).

13.23: $\sqrt[3]{100} < 5$ (because 5^3 is 125, which is greater than 100).

13.24: $8 < \sqrt{70} < 9$ (because 8^2 is 64 and 9^2 is 81, and 70 lies between these).

13.25: Three possibilities are $3 + 19$, or $5 + 17$, or $11 + 11$.

13.26: No. It is not possible to find two prime numbers that have a sum of 23.

13.27: $4 = 2 + 2$; $6 = 3 + 3$; $8 = 3 + 5$; $10 = 5 + 5$; $12 = 5 + 7$; $14 = 3 + 11$; $16 = 5 + 11$; $18 = 5 + 13$; $20 = 3 + 17$; $22 = 3 + 19$; $24 = 5 + 19$; $26 = 3 + 23$; $28 = 11 + 17$; $30 = 13 + 17$. Note that most of these can be done in more than one way. For example, $20 = 3 + 17$ or $7 + 13$.

13.28: Only those odd numbers that are equal to a prime number plus two, such as $21 (= 19 + 2)$.

13.29: The grower should put 120 flowers in each box. This is the lowest common multiple of 5, 8 and 12.

13.30: The smallest answer is 2520. This is the lowest common multiple of 1, 2, 3, 4, 5, 6, 7, 8, 9, 10.

13.31: This conjecture looks promising until you get to the nineties. There is only one prime number in the nineties, namely 97. If you think 91 is prime, try dividing it by 7.

13.32: The diagonal passes through 8 points on the grid.

13.33: The highest common factor of 16 and 24 is 8.

13.34: With a rectangle 15 units by 20 units, for example, the diagonal passes through 5 points on the grid.

13.35: The number of points on the grid the diagonal passes through is always the highest common factor of the two dimensions. In the case of the 16 by 24 rectangle, for example, you get from one corner to the other by moving 24 units horizontally and 16 units vertically. Because 8 is a common factor of 16 and 24, you could think of this as 8 steps along the diagonal, each equivalent to 3 units horizontally and 2 units vertically.

13.36: Sometimes. For example, $3^2 + 4^2$ is a square number ($= 25$); so are $6^2 + 8^2$ (100) and $5^2 + 12^2$ ($= 144$). But most sums of two square numbers are not square numbers. For example, $1^2 + 2^2$ ($= 5$) is not a square number, nor is $2^2 + 3^2$ ($= 13$).

13.37: Always. For example, $5^2 \times 7^2 = 35^2$ and $3^2 \times 11^2 = 33^2$. For those readers comfortable with algebraic generalizations, the general rule is $a^2 \times b^2 = (a \times b)^2$.

13.38: This is a remarkable pattern.

$1^3 = (1)^2$ [the first triangle number, 1, squared]

$1^3 + 2^3 = (1 + 2)^2$ [the second triangle number, 3, squared]

$1^3 + 2^3 + 3^3 = (1 + 2 + 3)^2$ [the third triangle number, 6, squared]

$1^3 + 2^3 + 3^3 + 4^3 = (1 + 2 + 3 + 4)^2$ [the fourth triangle number, 10, squared]

and so on.

In general, the sum of the first n cube numbers is the square of the nth triangle number. So, if, for example, you added up the first 100 natural numbers (to get 5050) and squared the answer (to get 25,502,500), this would be the sum of the first 100 cube numbers.

13.39: Whatever number is chosen, you should get the same result. In general, $(n^2)^3$ is equal to $(n^3)^2$.

13.40: The number is 64, which is 4 cubed and 8 squared.

13.41: These are some examples of what Jake may have been investigating:

- How many different ways can 18 be arranged in a rectangular array?
- Find pairs of factors of 18.
- Is 18 a prime number?
- What is the largest multiple of 6 less than 20?

13.42: Ask for some more examples of pairs of factors, using, say, 48. By questioning, help the children to formulate this hypothesis: 'all counting numbers have an even number of factors.' Ask how this might be investigated. Lead the children to check all numbers, starting with 2. Clearly, 1 has only one factor, but perhaps this is a special case? Are there other numbers with an odd number of factors? What are they? (1, 4, 9, 16, 25 and so on). Why do these have an odd number of factors? What's special about these? Reformulate the hypothesis: 'All whole numbers that are not … have an even number of factors.'

13.43: Plan A: I think this is the worst plan. It is better for a concept to be discovered through examples, rather than starting with a definition. It's a dull plan, with no context or purpose.

13.44: Plan B: This is a better plan, with the concept of prime number emerging gradually through examples and non-examples, and in the context of a game, which gives the activity some kind of purpose.

13.45: Plan C: This is the best plan, because it starts with a kind of real-life problem, so the concept of prime number emerges in a more meaningful context and in a task with some purpose.

13.46: All the following responses have come from Year 6 children:

- They are both square numbers.
- They both end in a 6.
- They are both even numbers.
- They are both multiples of 4.
- They both have 4 as a factor.
- They are both factors of 144.

- They are both less than 40.
- They are both more than 15.
- They both come between 15 and 37.
- They are both greater than 15.99999.
- They are both not prime numbers.
- They both have digits that add up to an odd number.
- They are both not in the 7-times table.
- They are both 10 away from 26.
- They both give remainder 1 when divided by 5.
- They are both whole numbers.
- They are both numbers in the question.

13.47: Because it has the possibility of many different kinds of response, this task encourages children to think divergently in mathematics. Children who come up with many different kinds of response show flexibility; those who come up with unusual (but appropriate) responses show originality. Flexibility and originality are two criteria for assessing creativity in mathematics.

13.48: The numbers represented are the odd numbers.

13.49: The diagram below shows how the shapes for 1, 3, 5 and 7 can be put together to make a 4 × 4 square array. We can see that $1 + 3 + 5 + 7 = 4^2$. Get children to use the same process to make a sequence of square arrays. For example, the shapes for 1, 3, 5, 7, 9, 11, 13, 15 (the first eight odd numbers) can be put together to make an 8 × 8 square array (8^2). Then look at the differences between successive square numbers: these produce the odd numbers.

13.50: The fourth option is CF.

13.51: For three activities (F, C, M) there are 9 options available: FF, FC, FM, CF, CC, CM, MF, MC and MM. This kind of problem encourages children to be systematic in order to cover every possibility.

13.52: Teach the children how to use a two-way table to make sure they have identified every possible combination, with the headings for the rows showing the first evening's choice and those for the columns the second evening's choice. The children could then construct a table to show all the permutations when there are four activities for each of the two evenings (there are 16 of them); and then five activities (for which there are 25 options). Discuss the patterns that emerge and help the children to see the square numbers involved and to articulate a rule.

	F	C	M
F	FF	FC	FM
C	CF	CC	CM
M	MF	MC	MM

13.53: Some children might then look at the number of possible options when there are two activities available over three nights. There are eight options: FFF, FFC, FCF, FCC, CFF, CFC, CCF, CCC. Then consider three activities over three nights (27 options), four activities over three nights (64 options) and five activities over three nights (125 options). Make the connection with cube numbers.

13.54: The number 1 is neither prime nor composite.

14.01: $(-7) < (-4)$

14.02: $(0) > (-4)$

14.03: $(+16) > (-20) > (-99)$

14.04: 7 °C (or +7 °C)

14.05: −22 pounds (or £22 overdrawn)

14.06: $(-8) + (+8) = 0$. Think of 8 steps in a negative direction followed by 8 steps in a positive direction.

14.07: $(-1) + (-3) + (-6) + (+8) = (-10) + (+8) = (-2)$

14.08: 14 °C

14.09: 4 °C

14.10: 12 °C

14.11: In the number line diagram shown below, Question 14.08 corresponds to the interval from −2 to 12; Question 14.09 to the interval from −6 to −2; Question 14.10 to the interval from −7 to 5.

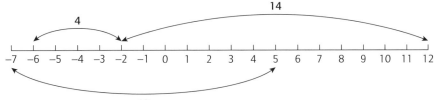

14.12: Question 14.08 corresponds to 12 − (−2) = 14; Question 14.09 corresponds to (−2) − (−6) = 4; and Question 14.10 corresponds to 5 − (−7) = 12. Note that 'the difference' is the same whichever of two temperatures is given first, but in calculating the difference the higher temperature goes first in the subtraction statement. The convention is to give the difference between two numbers as a positive number.

14.13: £8

14.14: £15

14.15: £7

14.16: In the number line diagram shown below, Question 14.13 corresponds to the step from 17 to 25; Question 14.14 to the step from −5 to 10; Question 14.15 to the interval from −12 to −5.

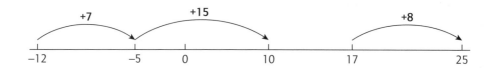

14.17: Question 14.13 corresponds to 25 − 17 = 8; Question 14.14 corresponds to 10 − (−5) = 15; and Question 14.15 corresponds to (−5) − (−12) = 7. Note that to find what must be added to b to make a, the subtraction is $a − b$.

14.18: The bottom of the Java Trench is the nearer, by about 470 metres. The calculation that corresponds to this is technically (−7130) − (−8600), but I expect, like me, you just did 8600 − 7130.

14.19: What is the difference in height between the bottom of the Puerto Rico Trench and the summit of Mount Everest? The answer is about 17,450 m.

14:20: Some suggestions:

• What is the difference in height between the bottom of the Marianas Trench and the summit of Mount McKinley? The answer is about 16,420 m. This could correspond to the subtraction 5500 − (−10,920) = 16,420.

• If you were at the bottom of the Marianas Trench, how much deeper would you be than someone at the bottom of the Java Trench? How much higher would they be than you? The answer to both questions is about 3790 m. The comparisons here could correspond to the subtraction (−7130) − (−10,920) = 3790.

14.21: The missing numbers, left to right from the top, are: 2, 10, −8, 1, −9, 7, −3, −1, −10, 5 and −11.

14.22: Three movements of four steps to the left are equivalent to 12 steps to the left. So a step of −4 done three times is a step of −12. In symbols, (−4) × 3 = −12. Any multiplication of a negative integer by a positive integer could be interpreted as a movement to the left done so many times.

14.23: Assuming that the *commutative* principle of multiplication works with negative numbers as well as positive, then 3 × (−4) must equal (−4) 3.

14.24 and 14.25: The completed table is as shown below:

×	−4	−3	−2	−1	0	1	2	3	4
−4	16	12	8	4	0	−4	−8	−12	−16
−3	12	9	6	3	0	−3	−6	−9	−12
−2	8	6	4	2	0	−2	−4	−6	−8
−1	4	3	2	1	0	−1	−2	−3	−4
0	0	0	0	0	0	0	0	0	0
1	−4	−3	−2	−1	0	1	2	3	4
2	−8	−6	−4	−12	0	2	4	6	8
3	−12	−9	−6	−3	0	3	6	9	12
4	−16	−12	−8	−4	0	4	8	12	16

14.26: The product of two negative integers is a positive integer. For example, (−3) × (−4) = 12.

14.27: There are two possible numbers, 4 or −4.

14.28: It will be on square 1.

14.29: Here is one suggestion. Use a number strip from, say, −15 to +15, with −12, −6, 0, 6 and 12 shaded. Have two dice, one conventional, and one marked −1 to −6. Start at zero, as before, and the first one to reach (or pass) 15 is the winner. Every third turn the players have to use the die with negative numbers. If you land on a shaded square when you have thrown a negative score, then 'go back 5 places' means moving in a positive direction.

14.30: The answer should be −3. Explain the subtraction as counting back 8 on a number line starting at 5. Use this model to emphasize that 5 − 8 and 8 − 5 do not give the same answer.

14.31: The answer should be −2. Starting at zero on a number line, interpret the 6 as a movement of 6 steps to the right and −8 as a movement of 8 steps to the left.

14.32: The answer should be 13. It is best to use the comparison idea of structure. What is the difference between 5 and −8 (for example, if these represent temperatures)? Illustrate the difference on a number line.

14.33: The answer should be 3. Again, use comparison and a number line. What is the difference between temperatures of −8 degrees and −5 degrees?

14.34: The answer should be −9. Perhaps discuss temperatures: think of this as the temperature starting at 0 °C, and then falling by 9 °C.

14.35 and 14.36: Suggest that the children's answers are reasonable and that the questions should have asked what the 'highest' and 'lowest' numbers are, rather than what the 'largest' and 'smallest' are. 'Higher' and 'lower' helpfully suggest positions on a vertical scale or number line. Talk about higher temperatures and lower temperatures, using a mix of positive and negative numbers. Make the point that 'a large negative number' (like −99 in this set) is a long way below zero, so it is a very low number. Use a number line to show that when we compare two numbers we always say that the 'greater' one is the one to the right, furthest in the positive direction. All the negative numbers are 'less than' zero on the number line (so 0 cannot be the lowest number in the given set) and all the positive numbers are 'greater than' zero.

15.01: $^2/_2 = {}^5/_5 = {}^{10}/_{10} = 1$; $^8/_{10} = {}^4/_5$; $^6/_{10} = {}^3/_5$; $^5/_{10} = {}^1/_2$; $^4/_{10} = {}^2/_5$; $^2/_{10} = {}^1/_5$

15.02: $^3/_5$ or $^6/_{10}$

15.03: $^5/_{10}$ or $^1/_2$

15.04: $^5/_{10}$ or $^1/_2$

15.05: $^3/_{10}$

15.06: Note that Questions 15.06–10 demonstrate some of the different meanings and representations of the fraction $^3/_8$. In Question 15.06 the fraction shaded is $^3/_8$ in each case.

15.07: Three-eighths of 32 children is 12 children, so the number of children who are not 8 years of age (five-eighths of them) is 20.

15.08: Each child gets $^3/_8$ of a square metre. The best way to see this is to divide the whole area into eight strips 3 metres long, as shown in the diagram. Each strip is made up of three bits, each of which is $^1/_8$ of a square metre.

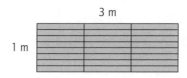

3 m

1 m

15.09: Amy has $^3/_8$ of the total amount, but the ratio of her share to Ben's share is 3:5.

15.10: Halfway between 0 and $^3/_4$ is the point $^3/_8$.

15.11: The possibilities include $^5/_8$, $^3/_5$, $^4/_7$ and $^{13}/_{20}$.

15.12: True. One twelfth of £36 is £3, so seven-twelfths is £21.

15.13: False ($^5/_6$ is $^{25}/_{30}$ and $^4/_5$ is $^{24}/_{30}$).

15.14: False. It is the denominator.

15.15: False. It is called an improper fraction.

15.16: True. If you multiply the top and bottom of $^5/_6$ by 15 you get $^{75}/_{90}$.

15.17: True.

15.18: True. Both are equivalent to 1:20.

15.19: False. The ratio is 1:2.

15.20: True. $^7/_{10}$ is equivalent to $^{28}/_{40}$ and $^3/_4$ is equivalent to $^{30}/_{40}$.

15.21: Pro rata, the first option is the better buy. Assume, for example, that all books cost £6 if bought individually. Then '3 for the price of 2' is equivalent to £4 for each book, while 'buy one get a second book half price' is £4.50 for each book. In practice, it depends on how many books you actually want to buy.

15.22: What it actually said implied that the prices in the sale were less than half price. So something originally priced at £100 could cost anything from £0 up to £50. However, I suspect it was intended to mean that the *reduction* was up to half price, so the £100 item could cost anything from £50 to £100.

15.23: When we use a fraction it must be clear what is the 'whole quantity' of which this is a part. The statement in this question is ambiguous because 'increased by a fifth' could refer to a fifth of the school population (which would be 40) or a fifth of the number having school lunches (which would be 16). In one case, it would mean the proportion of the population having school lunches had gone up from $^2/_5$ to $^3/_5$, an increase from 80 to 120. In the other case, it would mean an increase of 16 children having school lunches ($^1/_5$ of 80), taking the number from 80 to 96. This is a very common ambiguity.

15.24: Perhaps surprisingly, the number of children now on the school roll is not 275. This is because the 'fifths' are fifths of different numbers. The increase in the first year is $^1/_5$ of 275, which is 55, giving a total of 330. The decrease in the next year is $^1/_5$ of 330, which is 66, giving a total of 264.

15.25: (a) 7. (b) 12. (c) $^7/_{12}$. (d) The numerator is the sum of 3 and 4; the denominator is the product of 3 and 4.

15.26: The sum and product of 5 and 8 are 13 and 40. The sum of the two fractions $\frac{1}{5}$ and $\frac{1}{8}$ is $\frac{13}{40}$. This has a numerator that is the sum of 5 and 8, and a denominator that is the product of 5 and 8.

15.27: In general, $\frac{1}{a} + \frac{1}{b}$ is equal to a fraction with $(a + b)$ as the numerator and $(a \times b)$ as the denominator. This is, of course, prior to any cancellation that might then be done; for example, $\frac{1}{6} + \frac{1}{8} = \frac{14}{48}$, but this might then be cancelled down to $\frac{7}{24}$.

15.28: This problem-solving task requires some creative thinking. There are, in fact, 15 possibilities for the two missing numbers: 1 and 144, 2 and 72, 3 and 48, 4 and 36, 6 and 24, 8 and 18, 9 and 16, 12 and 12, 16 and 9, 18 and 8, 24 and 6, 36 and 4, 48 and 3, 72 and 2, and 144 and 1.

15.29: The two strips are lengths of 120 cm and 160 cm. If the original strip is divided into seven equal parts of 40 cm, then one cut strip will be three of these parts and the other will be four of them.

15.30: To generate the exact fractions given in the question, the number of children must be a common multiple of 7, 10, 4 and 3. The only such number less than 500 is 420. So there are 420 children: 120 having school dinners; 126 walking to school; 315 living within 2 miles; and 280 with 100% attendance.

15.31: Take a sheet of A4 paper. Fold it to show $\frac{2}{3}$ of the sheet. Do this in two different ways.

15.32: Draw a number line and mark two points as 0 and 1. Now put an arrow to show approximately where the number $\frac{2}{3}$ lies on your number line.

15.33: There are 27 children in this class. If $\frac{2}{3}$ of them are going on a school trip, how many of you will be going?

15.34: Working in threes, take 2 sheets of A4 paper and share them equally between you. What fraction of a sheet of A4 paper do you each get?

15.35: There are 50 children in this year group. There are 20 who walk to school and 30 who do not. Complete this sentence with a fraction: 'The number who walk to school is ... of the number who do not walk to school.' Give the fraction in its simplest form.

15.36: Congratulate the child on correctly representing $\frac{3}{4}$. Comment on the circle being divided into four equal parts, of which three are shaded. Then thank them for making a mistake that will help us to understand something important about fractions. Lead the child to see that the parts in the other diagram are not equal. For example, ask the child: If you like apple pie and this is an apple pie divided into six slices, which slice will you take? Why? Stress that in a fraction like $\frac{4}{6}$ the six parts must be equal.

15.37: This is a common category of error: manipulating mathematical symbols without any awareness of what they mean and what the manipulation represents. One way to help with this example is to use a 30-cm ruler to represent 'the whole thing'. First look at what would be half of the ruler, a third of the ruler and a fifth of the ruler. Is it possible that a half added to a third makes a fifth? Then use a fraction chart (with halves, thirds and sixths) to show that $\frac{1}{2} + \frac{1}{3} = \frac{3}{6} + \frac{2}{6} = \frac{5}{6}$.

15.38: Plan A is correct mathematically, but is a very abstract approach, encouraging children to manipulate symbols without making connections with anything concrete or visual; so this plan does not encourage children to engage with the meaning of what they are doing.

15.39: Plan B is good in connecting the symbols with real-life contexts. Plan B might have the edge as a starting point because it involves the children themselves in active participation, but it will need reinforcement in written form.

15.40: Plan C is also good in connecting the symbols with pictures and a real-life context. Plan B followed by Plan C and then Plan A would be a nice sequence of lessons.

15.41: If you answered 6, 8 and 3, then you have correctly recognized and applied a generalization. However, there are more creative solutions for 9 parts and 4 parts, using just 4 lines and 2 lines respectively.

15.42: The main point of this task is that it gives the child the opportunity to show that they can overcome a mental set. When we find a rule or process that works, it is often efficient to use it over and over again. But, if we use it without deviating from it, even when it is not necessarily the most interesting or elegant approach, then we are subject to a kind of fixation or rigidity which is the enemy of creative thinking. The essence of creativity in mathematics is to be flexible and divergent, rather than rigid and convergent.

16.01: 57.09, 57.9, 59.07, 75.09, 75.9, 79.05, 79.5

16.02: 0.00345, 0.0035, 0.00543, 0.03054, 0.04, 0.053, 0.3

16.03: See diagram below. Note that 0.209 is just less than 0.21.

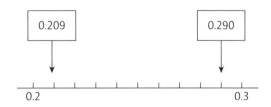

16.04: Approximately 3.914 and 3.998.

16.05: These blocks represent 34.3.

16.06: The length is 806 centimetres.

16.07: 8.06 metres.

16.08: On a calculator, $379 \div 49 = 7.7346938$. When rounded, this is 8 to the nearest whole number.

16.09: This is 7.7 to one decimal place.

16.10: To three significant digits, the result is 7.73.

16.11: To four decimal places, the result is 7.7347.

16.12: The calculator result is 17.533333. This means that 17 teams can be formed, with some children left over.

16.13: The figures after the decimal point (.533333) represent a fraction of a team.

16.14: The calculator result of 17.533333 means that the children get 17 pence each, with some money left over.

16.15: The figures after the decimal point (.533333) represent a fraction of a penny.

16.16: $263 \div 15 = 17$ with remainder 8.

16.17: In Question 16.12 the remainder 8 represents the eight remaining children not in a team.

16.18: In Question 16.14 the remainder 8 represents the 8p surplus that has not been shared between the children.

16.19: Correct.

16.20: Incorrect ($^7/_8 = 0.875$).

16.21: Incorrect ($^{23}/_{10} = 2.3$).

16.22: Correct.

16.23: Correct.

16.24: Incorrect ($^3/_5 = {}^6/_{10} = 0.6$).

16.25: The calculation to be entered on the calculator (the mathematical model for this problem) is $3000 \div 132$. The answer on my calculator (the mathematical solution) is 22.727272. The interpretation in the real world is that it will take me 23 months to reach (and pass) my target.

16.26: The calculation to be entered on the calculator (the mathematical model for this problem) is $3000 \div 96$. The answer on my calculator (the mathematical solution) is 31.25. The interpretation in the real world is that it will take me 32 months to reach (and pass) my target.

16.27: The calculator result for Question 16.25 (22.727272) is an answer (a recurring decimal) that has been truncated. The calculator answer to Question 16.26 (31.25) is an exact but inappropriate answer.

16.28: In both cases, in order to reach the target the calculator answers have had to be rounded up.

16.29: The mathematical model is 365 ÷ 7.

16.30: The solution is 52, remainder 1. The answer to Jo's problem is: there are 52 weeks in a (non-leap) year, plus one extra day. The remainder represents the one extra day.

16.31: The calculator solution is 52.142857. This is an answer that has been truncated.

16.32: The figures after the point represent a fraction of a week: they tell us that the one additional day is about 0.142857 of a whole week.

16.33: $3.45 \times 0.780 = 2.691$. The cost of the cheese is £2.69.

16.34: $15 \div 3.45 = 4.3478261$. You can buy just under 4.35 kg.

16.35: $8450 \div 3640 = 2.3214286$. It is about 2.3 times larger.

16.36: $325 \div 56 = 5.8035714$. So, 6 buses are required.

16.37: Clearly this data has been rounded. But how? It is not clear. Most of the numbers seem to be in millions rounded to two decimal places (so to the nearest ten thousand). So, for example, I would assume that the 16.15 million for 2008 represents an audience of somewhere between 16,145,000 and 16,155,000. But what do we make of the figures for 1986 and 1987? It *looks* as though the 30.1 million is rounded to only one decimal place (otherwise it would be given as 30.10 million) and the 28 million (not given as 28.0 or 28.00) *looks* as though it is rounded to the nearest whole number of millions. If that were the case, it would mean that the 28 million could represent an audience of anywhere between 27.5 million and 28.5 million. A correct procedure would have been to give all the data rounded to two decimal places, with two digits after the decimal point, using zeros where necessary.

16.38: If the 28 million means somewhere between 27.5 and 28.5 million, then we cannot tell whether the audience of 27.64 million is smaller than this. I suspect that the figures for 1986 and 1987 are in fact also rounded to two decimal places, in which case they should be given as 30.10 million and 28.00 million, to make this clear. These zeros are essential. An audience size given as 28.00 million would definitely be larger than one given as 27.64. Unless the data is correctly presented like this with the degree of rounding made clear, then it is impossible to compare figures sensibly. Dropping zeros after rounding throws away important information about the level of accuracy in the figures presented.

16.39: This short division calculation starts by dividing 10 (tenths) by 7. Once we reach the point where we have to divide 10 by 7 again, the same digits are going to recur in the answer. So, $^1/_7$ is equal to 0.142857… with the 142857 recurring.

$$0.\ 1\ 4\ 2\ 8\ 5\ 7\ 1\ …$$
$$7\ \overline{|1.\ {}^10\ {}^30\ {}^20\ {}^60\ {}^40\ {}^50\ {}^10\ …}$$

16.40: $^2/_7$ = 0.142857… + 0.142857… = 0.285714… (with the 285714 recurring).

16.41: $^3/_7$ = 0.285714… + 0.142857… = 0.428571… (with the 428571 recurring).

16.42: The same six digits recur in each of $^1/_7$, $^2/_7$ and $^3/_7$, but starting with a different digit each time. We could therefore predict that $^4/_7$, $^5/_7$ and $^6/_7$, respectively, will equal 0.571428… (with the 571428 recurring), 0.714285… (with the 714285 recurring) and 0.857142… (with the 857142 recurring). Check for yourself whether these predictions are correct.

16.43: The problems here are, first, that the calculator does not display unnecessary zeros after the point in decimal numbers, and, second, that in money notation the child interprets the point as just a separator between the pounds and the pence. Ask the child to calculate the cost of three items at £3.03 each on the calculator. What does this answer (9.09) mean? Note how it is different from 9.9. Explain that in 9.9 the calculator has thrown away the second zero and we have to put it back. Do some other examples to show this happening: for example, four items at £2.15 each.

16.44: This is a hangover from money notation where the point is used as just a separator between pounds and pence, where 'three pounds, forty-five (pence)' would be correct. Ask the child what the number 3.4 means: 3 ones and 4 tenths. Show this on the number line. Then show 3.5 and talk about dividing the space between them into ten equal parts. Each part is … ? A hundredth. Point to 3.45 and show that this is 3.4 and 5 hundredths. We say this as 'three point four five': three ones, four-tenths and five-hundredths. Follow up with other examples.

16.45: The child is not correct to draw this conclusion. This would be a good context for the child to begin to understand that if you do further calculations with rounded measurements then you can accumulate errors. One suggested way of helping the child is to give him an exaggerated example. Say there are 63 boys in a school and 65 girls. How many are there to the nearest 100? Answer: 100 of each. How many children altogether to the nearest 100? Is it 100 + 100 = 200? No, the answer is also 100. What's gone wrong? We have added two rounding errors and made a larger error. This can happen sometimes. Look at the actual example. If we had measured to the nearest centimetre, the length and width of the room might have been 7.49 m and 5.49 m. What would the perimeter then be? 7.49 + 7.49 + 5.49 + 5.49 = 25.96, which is 26 metres to the nearest metre. So, the answer of 24 metres could be as much as 2 metres out. Do the same with 6.51 m and 4.51 m.

16.46: The 3.10 should, of course, be 4 (or 4.0). Show the girl the way the questions are numbered in this book, saying that this is the kind of sequence that she is using, so her answer is perfectly reasonable. But these labels are not decimal numbers. A number line is the best way for her to see her error. Get her to mark points between 3.0 and 5.0 in tenths and label them. Then count in tenths from 3.4, going beyond 4.0. Repeat, starting at other points, such as 0.4 or 2.4.

16.47: A question with answer 4: 'There are 28 children in a class. For a game we need teams of 6. How many teams can we have?' A question with answer 5: 'There are 28 children in a class. We can get 6 children around a table. How many tables do we need?'

16.48: A question with answer 4: '£28 is available for buying books. The books cost £6 each. How many can we buy?' A question with answer 5: 'We need to raise £28. We can sell some books on eBay for £6 each. How many books must we sell to reach our target?'

16.49: The correct answer is 7.1428571 (approximately, of course). Both 250 ÷ 35 and 50 ÷ 7 give this answer on a calculator.

16.50: Praise the child for good understanding of equivalent ratios and thank her for making a mistake that helps us all to have a really useful mathematical discussion. Put the division into a context where a remainder would be meaningful. For example, 250 children in 35-seater buses requires how many buses? The calculation is 250 ÷ 35 = 7, remainder 5. That's 7 buses with 5 children remaining unseated. But the equivalent division, 50 ÷ 7, gives 7, remainder 1. What we learn is that we can't replace a division by an equivalent ratio if the answer is going to be given with a remainder. When she divided both numbers by 5 (to change 250 ÷ 35 into 50 ÷ 7), the remainder was divided by 5 as well.

17.01: My stride is 85 cm. So 24 paces is 24 × 85 cm = 2040 cm = 20.4 m (which is about the length of a cricket pitch).

17.02: The bottle holds 250 cl of water and a glass is 15 cl. So, the calculation is 250 ÷ 15 = 16, remainder 10. This means we can have 16 glasses of 15 cl, plus an additional glass with only 10 cl in it.

17.03: 3.985

17.04: 39,850

17.05: 4.683

17.06: 0.004683

17.07: Incorrect (100 − 65.43 = 34.57).

17.08: Correct.

17.09: Incorrect (0.095 × 2 = 0.19 which is less than 0.32).

17.10: Incorrect (9.06 ÷ 3 = 3.02).

17.11: Incorrect (10 ÷ 0.5 = 20). Ask yourself, for example, how many 0.5-litre bottles make 10 litres?

17.12: Incorrect. An approximation is 2.4 × 3 which equals 7.2, so the decimal point must be in the wrong place.

17.13: Incorrect (0.2 × 0.2 = 0.04).

17.14: Incorrect (this is equal to 2.5 million, so multiplication by one more 10 is required).

17.15: Incorrect (0.008 < 0.07).

17.16: Correct.

17.17: 320 ÷ 17 = 18, remainder 14.

17.18: To four decimal places, 320 ÷ 17 = 18.8235.

17.19: The relationship is that 0.8235 multiplied by 17 must equal 14 (allowing for the effect of a rounding error). Alternatively, 14 divided by 17 must equal 0.8235 (to four decimal places). This means that if the remainder of 14 could be shared equally between the 17, this would produce 0.8235 each (approximately). Whether or not this can actually be done in real life depends on the context that generated the division of 320 by 17.

17.20: One example is 'I have a 1.5-litre bottle of wine and pour out a glass of 0.125 litres. How much is left in the bottle?' (1500 ml subtract 125 ml is 1375 ml, so the answer is 1.375 litres.)

17.21: One example is 'What is the total mass of a 2.5-kg bag of potatoes and a 1.12-kg bag of onions?' (Answer: 2.500 + 1.120 = 3.620 kg.)

17.22: $A = 6.22$, $B = 2.56$, $C = 3.78$, $D = 9.88$, $E = 1.34$. Because $8.66 + 0.12 + A = E + 7.44 + A$, then $8.66 + 0.12$ must equal $E + 7.44$. So, $E + 7.44 = 8.78$, giving $E = 1.34$. From the three numbers in the leading diagonal, we can now deduce that the sum of each row, column or diagonal is $8.66 + 5 + 1.34 = 15$. The rest is relatively easy.

17.23: Because the result is less than 3, we can deduce that the 3.M5 has been multiplied by a number less than 1. Hence M is 0. Then we have 3.05 × 0.4, which equals 1.22, so N is 2.

17.24: If you divide 'six point something' by 'thirty something', the answer must be less than 1. So Q is 0. So, we have 6.P7 ÷ 30 = 0.P09. Since 6 ÷ 30 is 0.2, it seems likely that P is 2. This works: 6.27 ÷ 30 = 0.209.

17.25: My guess was 10. But a calculator gives $(0.9)^{10}$ as being 0.3874204. You actually need 22 of them multiplied together before you get a zero in the first decimal place of the answer.

17.26: The child has ignored the decimal point, so has added the 5 and the 2, the final digits in each number, then the 6 and the 3. The child needs reminding about what the digits after the decimal point represent: tenths and hundredths. Demonstrate with coins, with a pound representing 1, a ten-pence piece representing 0.1 (a tenth) and a penny representing 0.01 (a hundredth).

17.27: This is a common error. The child sees 8 – 3 first and gets the answer 5, then makes the 0.4 up to 1 by adding on 0.6. The child needs to think of the 3.4 as a complete number and to add on from 3.4 to 4 and then from 4 to 8.

17.28: The error is the result of a multiplication producing an answer with a zero at the end. If you calculate 326 × 5, the result is 1630. The answer for 3.26 × 0.5 must have three figures after the point, so it is 1.630. Encourage the child to estimate the answer first: what is 3 × 0.5?

17.29: The reasoning is probably: 8 ÷ 4 = 2, so 8 ÷ 0.4 = 0.2, which seems kind of logical if you don't think about what it all means. Encourage the child to think about the meaning of division: how many pieces of 0.4 of a pizza are there in 8 pizzas? Is 8 ÷ 0.4 larger or smaller than 8 ÷ 4? Stress the principle that if you divide by a smaller number, the answer is larger.

17.30: Three typical questions would be to calculate 0.25 × 1000 (= 250), 8 ÷ 100 (= 0.08), and 0.25 ÷ 10 (= 0.025).

17.31: Three typical questions would be to calculate 0.4 × 12 (= 4.8), 2.05 × 3 (= 6.15), and 0.15 × 120 (= 18).

17.32: Three typical questions would be to calculate 4.5 ÷ 15 (= 0.3), 0.56 ÷ 7 (= 0.08), and 12 ÷ 25 (= 0.48).

17.33: The whole rectangle represents 5 × 8 (= 40). This is divided up into 10 strips each of 0.8 units wide. The shaded strip represents 5 × 0.8, which is $\frac{1}{10}$ of 40 = 4.

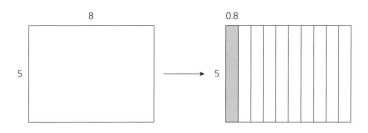

17.34: The rectangle is now divided up into 10 vertical strips each of 0.8 units wide and 10 horizontal strips each of 0.5 units wide. The shaded rectangle in the top left-hand corner represents 0.5 × 0.8, which is $^1/_{100}$ of 40 = 0.4.

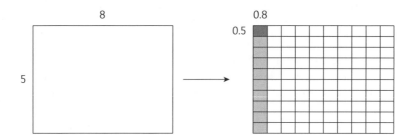

17.35: Discuss with the children how the area of the rectangle is made up of two sections and what multiplications they represent (3 × 0.40 and 3 × 0.02). Help them to work out each multiplication, perhaps relating it to calculations with money (3 items at £0.40 and 3 items at £0.02), and to record the results carefully: 3 × 0.40 = 1.20 and 3 × 0.02 = 0.06, giving (by addition) 3 × 0.42 = 1.26.

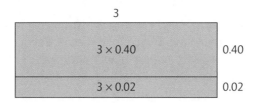

17.36: Discuss with the children how the area of the rectangle is made up of four sections and what multiplications they represent (30 × 0.40, 6 × 0.40, 30 × 0.02 and 6 × 0.02). Help them to work out each multiplication, perhaps again relating it to money calculations (30 items at £0.40 and so on). Encourage them to record the results carefully: 30 × 0.40 = 12.00, 6 × 0.40 = 2.40, 30 × 0.02 = 0.60 and 6 × 0.02 = 0.12; giving 36 × 0.42 = 12.00 + 2.40 + 0.60 + 0.12 = 15.12.

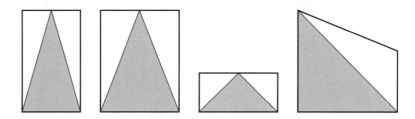

18.01: For 4 cakes we need 50 g, so for 12 cakes we need 50 g multiplied by 3. So, for 12 cakes, we need 150 g of peanuts.

18.02: For 4 cakes we need 50 g, so for 2 cakes we need 25 g. So, for 10 cakes, we need 50 g + 50 g + 25 g = 125 g of peanuts.

18.03: For 10 cakes we need 125 g, so for 2 cakes we need 25 g. Then, for 4 cakes, we need 50 g of cocoa.

18.04: For 6 cakes we need 220 grams, so for 1 cake we need (220 ÷ 6) grams. So, for 11 cakes, we need 11 × (220 ÷ 6) grams, which is about 400 grams of flour (11 × 220 ÷ 6 = 403 approximately).

18.05: 528 out of 1200 is the same proportion as 264 out of 600.

18.06: 264 out of 600 is the same proportion as 132 out of 300.

18.07: 132 out of 300 is the same proportion as 44 out of 100.

18.08: So, the proportion of over-50s in the village is 44%.

18.09: $^3/_4$ = 0.75 = 75%

18.10: 37% = 0.37 = $^{37}/_{100}$

18.11: $^3/_{20}$ (= $^{15}/_{100}$) = 0.15 = 15%

18.12: 0.16 = 16% = $^{16}/_{100}$, which is $^4/_{25}$ in its simplest form.

18.13: 1% = 0.01 = $^1/_{100}$

18.14: $^6/_{25}$ (= $^{24}/_{100}$) = 0.24 = 24%

18.15: 0.1% is a tenth of 1%; since 1% is equivalent to 0.01, 0.1% must be equivalent to 0.001, or $^1/_{1000}$.

18.16: It makes no difference. In one case, the calculation could be 600 × 1.20 × 0.90; in the other case, it could be 600 × 0.90 × 1.20. The result is the same: £648.

18.17: Intuitively you may think my shares are back to the £5000. First, 20% of £5000 is £1000, taking the value of my investment down to £4000. But then the increase in value will be 20% of this £4000, which is only £800. So my shares are now worth £4800.

18.18: Rob wants to make a monthly gift worth £200 to the charity. If he gives 80% of this amount, then the government gives the 20% tax they have already deducted from Rob. So, Rob gives £160 a month (80% of £200) and the charity gets the £200 a month.

18.19: This is tricky. Jan gives £5400 per annum to the charity. But 20% of the gross amount she earned to produce this £5400 has already been deducted. So, the £5400 is actually 80% of the gross earnings. The mathematical problem is: if 80% is £5400, what is 100%? An easy way of working this out is first to find

10%, by dividing £5400 by 8. This gives £675. So, 100% is £6750. So Jan's annual gift of £5400 is actually worth £6750 to the charity. This is why charities love gift aid.

18.20:   Imagine the article costs £100. The reduced price is £80. The 'further 10%' should mean 10% of the original price, making the price £70. But it probably means 10% of the reduced price, making the price £72. So, the total reduction might be only 28%, not 30% as we might expect.

18.21:   This is a common problem when people talk about percentages of percentages. Say the share of the vote is 40%. Going up by 10% might mean going up to 50%, or going up to 44%. In one case, the increase is 10% of the total vote; in the other, it is 10% of their share of the vote. We have no way of knowing which is intended, although they will probably mean the second but want us to think the first. To avoid this confusion, people who are careful about these things say 'an increase of 10 percentage points' when they mean going up from 40% to 50%.

18.22:   This is another example where it is not clear what the percentage refers to. If it actually meant 49% of the number of patients having surgery on Friday then this would really be 'soaring', from 0.55% on Monday to 49.55% on Friday. But it does not. It means a 49% increase in the *proportion* of patients dying: in other words, a percentage of a percentage. The proportion of patients who die after surgery on a Monday is 0.55% which increases to 0.82% after a Friday operation (49% of 0.55% is 0.27% while 0.55% + 0.27% = 0.82%). So, a patient has 99.18% and 99.45% chances of surviving Friday and Monday operations respectively. Both are extremely high chances and the survival rate for Mondays is only slightly better than that for Fridays. If I needed surgery, I would be grateful to take either.

18.23:   To analyse this statement, using the words 'failed' and 'succeeded' as a convenient, but inappropriate, shorthand, we consider four groups of children:

A: those who failed in English and failed in maths

B: those who failed in English and succeeded in maths

C: those who succeeded in English and failed in maths

D: those who succeeded in English and succeeded in maths.

The statement could then mean any of the following:

50% failed both subjects (50% of children are in group A)

50% failed in each subject (A + C = 50% of the children; and A + B = 50% of the children)

50% did not succeed in both subjects (A + B + C = 50% of the children).

As it happens, none of these was true. The headline was a complete fabrication by the newspaper.

18.24: The child has treated 5% as meaning a fifth. This is probably because 10% is a tenth. Make the point strongly that 10% being equal to a tenth is a unique case. But we can use it to work out other percentages. We know that 10% of £40 is £4, so what will be 5%? 5% is half of 10% …

18.25: The child is confusing 20% with £20. This might just be a careless misreading of the question, rather than a significant misunderstanding. Again, ask how much would be 10% of £60 and use this to work out 20%.

18.26: The increase is 20% of £50, but not 20% of the original price. Remind the children that we must always ask this question about a percentage: what is it a percentage of? In this case, we should think of the £10 increase as a percentage of the original price of £40 (a 25% increase).

18.27: This approach is mathematically sound, but it is very didactic, and because it relies on changing the percentage into an equivalent fraction, it requires a lot of confidence in handling fraction calculations.

18.28: I like this approach, because it is based on the principle of using what you know to find what you don't yet know. We know 10% of £40 – it is always easy to work out 10% of anything. From that we can work out percentages such as 5% and 20% and then piece them together to get, in this case, 35%. It is surprising how many everyday percentage calculations can be done in this informal way. It is worth encouraging.

18.29: Some questions to ask: 50% of what? Half price? What does 50% mean? How do we say this as a fraction? Use various examples, such as trousers costing £20, or a top costing £14. Compare with other reductions, such as 20% off or a third off.

18.30: Ask how this data might have been collected. How many people do we think were asked? Discuss what would have been a good sample. What are the meanings of 9% and 91%? What do we make of the fact that 9% added to 91% equals 100%? What does 100% mean? What happened to those who said 'don't know'? Is it a good idea to ignore them?

18.31: Discuss the idea of a no claims bonus, drawing on any experience children may have of this. Talk about this being a common use of percentages in everyday life. Which is better? A 50% no claims bonus or a 75% no claims bonus? Why? What does 75% mean? What is this as a fraction? If the original insurance premium was £400, what would be the bonus? So how much would you pay? Compare this with other bonus rates, such as 50% or 60%.

18.32: Ask whether a 5% tax cut sounds like a lot or a little. Have a discussion about how income tax works and how the rates always use percentages, often expressed as 'so much in the pound'. Make the connection strongly: 25% tax is 25p in the pound. Take the example of someone earning £35,000 a year, of which £5000 is tax free. Work through how much tax they pay at 25% and how much if this is reduced to 20%. How much is the 5% cut in tax worth to this person? Is that more than the children expected?

18.33: Discuss what 'commission' means. How does 20% commission on a sale compare with 10% commission? What commission would you get on a sale of £200? Repeat with other amounts, encouraging the learners to find 10% and then double it. What sale would be necessary for a commission of £10? What about a commission of 25% …?

19.01: The output is 46.

19.02: The output set is {0, 2, 4, 6, 8, … 98} (even numbers from 0 to 98 inclusive).

19.03: mapping

19.04: independent

19.05: dependent

19.06: formula

19.07: function

19.08: £23 for 3 books. £125 for 20 books.

19.09: £$(6n + 5)$

19.10: £53 is the cost of 8 books.

19.11: $6n + 5 = 53$.

19.12: The total number of items bought (xylophones and yo-yos).

19.13: The number of yo-yos multiplied by 3, which is the cost of the yo-yos in pounds.

19.14: The number of xylophones multiplied by 8 plus the number of yo-yos multiplied by 3, which is the total cost in pounds of all the items bought.

19.15: The choice of letters for the variables here could reinforce the misconception that they are abbreviations for the objects (for example, x could be perceived as an abbreviation for a xylophone and y for a yo-yo), instead of variables (x is the number of xylophones and y the number of yo-yos). So $8x + 3y$ might be wrongly thought to stand for 8 xylophones and 3 yo-yos. Apologies if I misled you into giving the wrong answers. Well done if you avoided the trap.

19.16: The m here is an abbreviation for a metre. It is not a variable.

19.17: The *m* here is a variable, meaning 'any number of cars'. Notice the convention of using italics for a letter that represents a variable.

19.18: The m here is just a label (such as an abbreviation for a teacher's surname), without any particular mathematical significance.

19.19: The number 5 units to the left of *n* is *n* – 5. When *n* = −3 this has the value −8. When *n* = 2 this has the value −3.

19.20: It depends. If *n* is a negative number then 5*n* will be to the left of *n*. If *n* is a positive number then 5*n* will be to the right of *n*. And what if *n* is zero?

19.21: The easiest way of expressing this number is $\frac{1}{2}(n + 20)$, but there are other formulas equivalent to this. When *n* = 50 this has the value 35. When *n* = −10 this has the value 5.

19.22: The numbers are 3*n* and −*n*.

19.23: Either *q* < *n* < *p* or *p* > *n* > *q*.

19.24: True. Since *p* and *q* can each be any of 1, 2, 3, 4, 5, 6, 7, 8 or 9, then 10*p* + *q* will be a whole number from 11 to 99, excluding multiples of 10.

19.25: The two possible solutions are *p* = 4, *q* = 3; and *p* = 9, *q* = 2.

19.26: The two possible solutions are *p* = 3, *q* = 2; and *p* = 7, *q* = 5.

19.27: The only solution is *p* = 9, *q* = 8.

19.28: For one sheet, the centre pages are 2 and 3; for two sheets, 4 and 5; for three sheets, 6 and 7; for four sheets, 8 and 9.

19.29: 100 and 101.

19.30: 2*n* and 2*n* + 1.

19.31: When *a* = 10 and *b* = 70, the formula gives *x* = 40, which is halfway between 10 and 70.

19.32: When *a* = 10 and *b* = 70, *y* would be 30. The simplest formula is $y = \frac{1}{3}(2a + b)$, but you may come up with an equivalent formula that looks different from this.

19.33: When *a* = 10 and *b* = 70, *z* would be 25. The simplest formula is $z = \frac{1}{4}(3a + b)$.

19.34: The simplest formula is $p = \frac{1}{6}(5a + b)$. When *a* = 10 and *b* = 70, for example, this gives *p* = 20.

19.35: The result is 228.

19.36: My number was 10.

19.37: My number was 3.4. (It could also have been −5, but I did not expect you to get that. Well done if you did.)

19.38: The equation being solved is $x(5x + 8) = 85$.

19.39: Most children in Years 5 and 6 would be able to identify the pattern and continue the sequence in row B by adding 3 each time. In doing this they recognize the sequential generalization. More able children would be able to articulate a rule for getting from the number in A to the number in B: multiply by 3 and add 1. This is the global generalization. The most able children may be able to write this algebraically: $b = 3a + 1$, for example.

19.40: Finding the number in row B to be 301 directly from the 100 in row A would be a good indicator of the child having identified the global generalization. Other children will laboriously try to count on in threes from the last result in row B.

19.41: The child who puts 34 in the final box under the 100 is not relating the numbers in row B to those in row A at all.

19.42: The children have to treat the number on the card as a variable, because it could take any value. In essence, they are solving an equation, such as $x + 3 = 7$, trying to find the value of x that makes this true. The number on the card is an independent variable. The number the teacher says is a dependent variable, being dependent on the number on the card and determined by the 'add 3' rule.

19:43: The activity can be developed by using different rules. The teacher could do one or two more rules (such as 'now I'm the subtract two person' or 'now I'm the doubling person'). Children in turns could then be asked to be the 'add one person' and so on. Another development would be to show the children the numbers on the cards drawn, and call out the result of using the rule. The children then have to find the rule. This involves generalization, the essence of algebraic thinking.

19.44: Always true, because we are told they each have some money.

19.45: Never true, because $x + y$ must be equal to 85.

19.46: Sometimes true; when John has more than Sarah.

19.47: Here are my three examples: (i) $2x + 2y = 170$; (ii) $x < 85$; (iii) $85 - x = y$.

19.48: Here are my three examples: (i) $2x = y$; (ii) $x < 10$; (iii) $y - x = 10$.

19.49: Here are my three examples: (i) $x = y$; (ii) $x > 100$; (iii) $y < 1$.

19.50: The correct solution is $x = 12$.

19.51: The child has clearly interpreted $18 + 4x$ as 'add 18 and 4 and then multiply by x'. If you enter '18 + 4 × 3 =' onto a basic calculator you get the answer 66. Show this to the child and remind them that these calculators don't know that you have to do the multiplication first. But we do. Perhaps show what happens on a calculator with an algebraic operating system. Explain that the convention is that 18 + 4*x* means 18 + (4*x*). The 4*x* must be calculated first. Try some other inputs using the correct precedence of operators.

20.01: True.

20.02: True. This equation gives a straight-line graph.

20.03: False. The equation is not satisfied by $a = 0$, $b = 0$.

20.04: True.

20.05: False. For example, if y is equal to 3*x*, then when $x = 1$, $y = 3$. Increase x by 5 so $x = 6$. Then $y = 18$. So y has increased by 15, not 5.

20.06: False. For example, (15, 12) lies on the graph of $y = x + 3$, but (5, 4) does not.

20.07: True. The equation of the graph is $5y = 4x$.

20.08: Not directly proportional. A simple test for direct proportionality is: 'if you double x, must you necessarily double y?' This is not the case with postage costs. A 20-gram package will not cost twice as much as a 10-gram package.

20.09: Allowing for small rounding errors and provided there are no special offers, we would normally expect y to be directly proportional to x in this example.

20.10: Allowing for small rounding errors, we would normally expect y to be directly proportional to x in this example.

20.11: Not directly proportional. You could increase the number of children by 2, for example, and the number of teachers would probably not change.

20.12: Not directly proportional. Double your speed from 20 mph to 40 mph, for example, and the stopping distance is increased from 12 metres to 36 metres, which is three times greater.

20.13: Not directly proportional. The ball slows down as it gets higher, so the increase in height is not proportional to the time.

20.14: This is an example of direct proportionality. The perimeter of a square is always 4 times the length of one side.

20.15: Not directly proportional. For example, if you double the length of the side of a square from 5 to 10 centimetres, the area increases by a factor of 4, from 25 to 100 square centimetres.

20.16: Not directly proportional. For example, a 10-minute job costs £30, but the cost of a 20-minute job is not double this (i.e. not £60).

20.17: Questions 20.09, 20.10 and 20.14, where the relationship is direct proportionality, are the only examples in which we would expect a straight-line graph passing through the origin.

20.18: Of the graphs identified in Q20.17 the only one in which all the points on the graph have meaning is Question 20.14. In Questions 20.09 and 20.10, at least one of the variables is limited to whole number values (pence or rupees).

20.19: 82 °F is about 28 °C; 16 °C is about 61 °F. Because all you have to do is to reverse the digits, these two conversions are very easy to remember.

20.20: We can tell immediately that the temperatures in °C and °F are not directly proportional because the graph does not pass through the origin (0 °C does not equal 0 °F).

20.21: The possible positions for C in the first quadrant are (5, 3) and (3, 1).

20.22: The possible positions for C in the second quadrant are (–3, 3) and (–1, 1).

20.23: The possible position for C in the third quadrant is (–3, –1); and in the fourth quadrant, (5, –1).

20.24: It becomes a non-rectangular parallelogram, with the same height and the same base as the original rectangle.

20.25: This process produces a sequence of parallelograms, all with the same height and base as the original rectangle (and the same area).

20.26: The fourth vertex could be (1, 3), (1, –1) or (7, 5).

20.27: The sum of the x-coordinates of one pair of opposite vertices is equal to the sum of the x-coordinates of the other pair. The same applies to the y-coordinates.

20.28: Latitude 35° South (of the equator) and longitude 58° West (of the Greenwich meridian).

20.29: Where the Greenwich meridian crosses the equator. This is somewhere warm in the Atlantic Ocean, about 380 miles south of Ghana and 670 miles west of Gabon.

20.30: The 90° North latitude puts you at the North Pole, regardless of what longitude is stated.

20.31: Edinburgh.

20.32: The coordinates would be (–56, +177), which is somewhere cold in the South Pacific Ocean, between New Zealand and Antarctica.

20.33: Here are three suggestions: (i) a room where seats are arranged in rows and columns, such as seating in the hall for a school concert; (ii) cells on a spreadsheet or any two-way table or array, such as a school timetable; and (iii) the paper-and-pencil game sometimes called 'battleships and cruisers'.

20.34: In these examples, the two coordinates identify a space, an area or a cell in a grid. Familiar examples like these are a useful introduction to how coordinate systems use two-way reference. But the transition to a Cartesian coordinate system, in which the two coordinates identify a specific point, will require careful explanation by the teacher.

20.35: It could be placed in any of the rows in the 3rd or 4th cells along.

20.36: Two-digit numbers less than 12. Only two possibilities are 10 and 11.

20.37: The game develops the child's ability to make two-way references, which is the basis of a coordinate system. For each cell they have to check the criteria for both the row and the column.

20.38: Simpler or more challenging labels for the rows and columns; a smaller or a larger grid; fewer or more number cards; for older children, number cards in a greater range, such as 30–60.

20.39: The coordinates are (0, −2), (0, −5), (5, −9) and (3, 0).

20.40: These are some ideas for an extended activity along these lines. Discuss in what ways the two quadrilaterals A and B are the same and how they are different. Discuss the symmetry of the whole figure. Then get them to reflect quadrilateral A in the *y*-axis to produce quadrilateral C. Have a similar discussion about quadrilaterals A and C, and about quadrilaterals B and C. Put the children in pairs and get one child to reflect quadrilateral B in the *y*-axis and the other to reflect quadrilateral C in the *x*-axis. What do they discover when they compare their results? (They are the same: call this quadrilateral D.) Ask how quadrilateral A could be transformed into quadrilateral D in one go (by a rotation through 180 degrees). Discuss the symmetry of the whole drawing. Lots of good mathematics here. Repeat it with other starting shapes.

20.41: A convention is an arbitrary rule, required just to avoid potential confusion – like everyone agreeing to drive on the left. There is little to *understand* as such, just a rule to learn, to remember and to follow. But a concept is learnt by experience of a number of exemplars of the concept, comparing these with non-exemplars, and gradually clarifying what it is that the various exemplars of the concept have in common. Understanding a concept involves making connections between the different exemplars and connections with relevant mathematical language and symbols. If I am to learn a concept, I need a teacher to plan experiences through which I can make connections and gradually build up conceptual understanding. To learn a convention I just need someone to tell me what it is, show me how it works and help me to remember it. A little aide-memoire like 'along the hall then up the stairs' is often used to give quasi-meaningfulness to the convention of coordinates.

21.01: The quantity of water that a container can hold is called the capacity of the container.

21.02: Both volume and capacity can be measured in litres.

21.03: The gravitational force that pulls an object downwards is called its weight.

21.04: The SI unit for measuring weight is the newton.

21.05: A kilogram is a measure of mass.

21.06: The mass of an object does not change when its distance from the earth's centre changes.

21.07: Two different aspects of time are recorded time, such as 12:30 p.m, and a time interval, such as 8 seconds.

21.08: If A → B and B → C then A → C.

21.09: Ali is shorter than Carl.

21.10: Transitive.

21.11: Transitive.

21.12: Not transitive. If three objects A, B and C are 400 g, 200 g and 100 g respectively, then A is twice as heavy as B, B is twice as heavy as C, but A is not twice as heavy as C.

21.13: Transitive.

21.14: Transitive.

21.15: Not transitive. Nottingham is nearer to Birmingham than it is to London; London is nearer to Birmingham than it is to Derby; but Nottingham is not nearer to Birmingham than it is to Derby.

21.16: Transitive.

21.17: 0.02 km, the length of your arm, 15 inches, 15 cm.

21.18: Half a stone, 0.5 kg, the mass of a small packet of crisps, 1200 mg.

21.19: Sorry, trick question! These are all the same.

21.20: The volume of 2.5 kg of water (which is 2.5 litres), 0.75 litres, the capacity of a can of drink (usually 330 ml), 80 ml.

21.21: An estimate between 4.5 and 6.5 metres is reasonable.

21.22: About 350 days. It's about 25,000 miles, which would take about 8,333 hours.

21.23: An estimate between 12 kg and 18 kg is pretty good. Sand is clearly heavier than water (it doesn't float when the tide comes in) and 10 litres of water has a mass of 10 kg.

21.24: Most children reach the height of 1 metre between their 3rd and 4th birthdays.

21.25: Weight is the force of gravity pulling an object down towards the ground. Pressure is the weight per unit of area. There's more pressure if all the weight of an object is concentrated on a small area than when it is spread out over a larger area. If the object is sitting on my hand, the pressure could be measured in newtons (units of weight) per square centimetre, for example. The pressure on my hand is the weight of the object divided by the area of contact between my hand and the object.

21.26: The book may feel lighter because the weight is distributed over a larger area – you may be more conscious of the pressure on your hand than the weight of the object. Putting the two objects in carrier bags removes the distraction of the pressure on your hand. This is a really good tip for getting children to compare the weights of objects by hand.

21.27: This is a consequence of the fact that any measurement is approximate. European legislation specifies the tolerance allowed for any given quantity and product. With this symbol, the manufacturer guarantees that they are meeting the requirements of this legislation.

21.28: 330 ml × 6 = 1980 ml = 1.98 litres, so we might think the 6 cans contain less than the bottle. However, because the 330 ml and the 2 litres are approximate measurements guaranteeing at least 330 ml and 2 litres within accepted levels of tolerance, six cans could contain less or more than the volume of drink in the 2-litre bottle.

21.29: Place the 3-g mass in Pan A as well, then the 7-g mass in Pan B. Add sand until the two pans balance.

21.30: The most common responses to this task are:

(16, 7, 3 row) 16 and 3 in A, 7 in B

(2, 50, 40 row) 50 and 2 in A, 40 in B

(5, 55, 50 row) 55 and 5 in A, 50 in B

(14, 11, 3 row) 14 and 3 in A, 11 in B

(81, 7, 8 row) 81 and 7 in A, 8 in B

(55, 10, 5 row) 55 and 10 in A, 5 in B

(7, 6, 10 row) 7 and 6 in A, 10 in B

(30, 20, 8 row) 30 and 8 in A, 20 in B

(32, 20, 8 row) 32 and 8 in A, 20 in B

These are all correct. However, if you have these answers, ask yourself why you did not just put the 20-g mass in the last example in Pan A to measure out 20 g of sand in Pan B? This task is a powerful illustration of the way in which we get stuck into using rules and recipes in mathematics and stop thinking about what things actually mean. The first few examples are deliberately designed to establish a mental set, a fixation on one way of doing these questions, which most people use for all of them. If you got 20 g in Pan A for the last example, then well done for showing flexibility in thinking. Bonus praise for flexible thinking if you put just 55 and 5 in pan A in the (55, 10, 5) row, and if you put 10 in pan A and 7 in pan B in the (7, 6, 10) row.

21.31: Start by talking about any experiences they may have of playing on seesaws with much bigger or much smaller children. Then get the children to hold two objects where one is clearly much heavier than the other: a good example would be two identical yogurt pots, one filled with ball bearings and the other filled with polystyrene bits. Talk about heavier and lighter. Put the objects in the pans and see which one goes down: the heavier one. Now look at the playdough in the scales and ask the obvious questions: Which lump is heavier? Which lump is lighter?

21.32: Get the children to change the shape of one of the lumps in some way (for example, make a sausage shape or a model of a person) and compare the two pieces again in the scales. Break one of the lumps up into several smaller pieces and compare them again. Talk about the fact that the shape changes but it does not get any heavier or any lighter – because it still balances the other lump.

21.33: If you get to 11:25 a.m. in the bottom right-hand corner, you know you have this correct. For reference, the bottom row should read: 9:20 a.m., 9:45 a.m., 10:10 a.m., 10:35 a.m., 11:00 a.m., 11:25 a.m.

21.34: Obviously this same grid could be used with different starting and finishing times, cutting across a.m. and p.m., for example. It could be used with different time notation, such as the 24-hour clock. And you can vary the instructions for moving from one cell to the next. It could also be used for any measuring context. For example, for capacity the instructions could be something like 'holds 50 ml more' and 'holds 75 ml less', starting with 1 litre. For mass, they could be '250 g heavier' and '200 g lighter', starting with 1 kg. For length, you could use 'increase by 20 cm' and 'decrease by 15 cm', starting with 1 metre.

21.35: In practice, once children have learnt to use these grids, I recommend that you have a supply of them available for each measuring context to be used as a 'filler' when the children have completed the tasks you have planned for a lesson. Grids can also be used, for example, for the addition and subtraction of whole numbers, decimals and even simple fractions.

21.36: This is a common error in the early stages of learning to use a ruler for measuring length. Give Liam a measuring strip or ruler that does not extend to the left beyond zero (make one out of card?). It helps then to do the measuring vertically so the pencil stands on the table next to the measuring strip. Also, emphasize the idea of conservation of length. Cut a strip of paper 6 cm long, dividing it up with lines into centimetre-long sections. Move this along the ruler to different positions and get Liam to count how many sections there are and to observe that it always stays as 6 cm in length.

21.37: Lou makes an accurate observation, but is answering a different question. What the teacher sees as significant is not what Lou sees. Ask Lou to fill the larger container and try to pour the contents into the smaller container, and then have another discussion about which holds more.

21.38: Jon is also making an accurate observation: namely that the two ends of line B are the same distance apart horizontally as are the two ends of line A. To focus on the lengths of A and B, ask him to measure the length of line B with a piece of string and lay it along line A. Think of them as paths: which would be the longer walk?

21.39: Jack is to be congratulated on his mental arithmetic: instantly doubling 26 to get 52. It should be easy enough to show him that lifting one leg when you are standing on scales does not alter the reading shown on the scales. He probably needs some explanation about all the weight going down one leg when you lift the other one. This is a genuine account: the next thing Jack did was to lie on the floor and put his head on the scales to see how much his head weighs. Unfortunately, when he lifted his head to read the weight, the scales returned to zero.

21.40: See Questions 21.25 and 21.26. Megan is responding to the pressure rather than the weight of the objects. In the box all the weight is concentrated on a small area of her hand, making it appear heavier. Obviously get out the weighing scales and (if possible, with the large lump of polystyrene) some balance scales. Then give Megan some other, similar examples of large and small, heavy and light objects to compare.

21.41: Atiano is speaking on 1 January, the day after her 11th birthday on 31 December.

21.42: Here's one way of getting 4 litres in the larger bottle.

Fill the 5-litre bottle.

(now 0 litres in small, 5 litres in large)

Use 5-litre bottle to fill 3-litre bottle.

(now 3 litres in small, 2 litres in large)

Empty 3-litre bottle.

(now 0 litres in small, 2 litres in large)

Pour contents of 5-litre bottle into 3-litre.

(now 2 litres in small, 0 litres in large)

Fill 5-litre bottle.

(now 2 litres in small, 5 litres in large)

Top up 3-litre bottle from 5-litre bottle.

(now 3 litres in small, 4 litres in large, as required)

21.43: On a 12-hour clock, what time will it be 4 hours after 9 pm?

21.44: On a 12-hour clock, what time will it be 8 hours after 9 o'clock on the evening before the start of British Summer Time (Daylight Saving Time)?

22.01: The area of shape (a) is 10 square units.

22.02: The perimeter of shape (b) is 18 units.

22.03: Shape (b) has the largest area, 12 square units.

22.04: Shape (a) has the smallest area, 10 square units.

22.05: Shape (a) has the greatest perimeter, 22 units.

22.06: Shape (c) has the smallest perimeter, 14 units.

22.07: They can be rearranged to make a rectangle, 3 units by 4 units; this has the smallest possible perimeter (14 units).

22.08: $0.6 \times 0.6 = 0.36$, so the area is 0.36 square metres.

22.09: $60 \times 60 = 3600$, so the area is 3600 square centimetres.

22.10: $20 \times 15 \times 25 = 7500$, so the volume is 7500 cubic centimetres.

22.11: $0.20 \times 0.15 \times 0.25 = 0.0075$, so the volume is 0.0075 cubic metres. Remember that 1 cubic metre is 1 million cubic centimetres.

22.12: 10 m; area = 160 m^2.

22.13: 22 m; area = 88 m^2.

22.14: 13 m by 13 m (a square); area = 169 m^2.

22.15: False, because $0.8 \times 0.8 = 0.64$. The length of the side of the square is 0.4 m, because $0.4 \times 0.4 = 0.16$, as required.

22.16: True. This is easy to see if you convert the lengths to centimetres. The length of the side of the square is 25 cm and that of the blocks is 5 cm.

22.17: False. Only 20 containers are required; the capacity of one container is 0.05 m^3. Note that 20 multiplied by 0.05 is 1.

22.18: The triangles required are shown below. If you got the last one wrong, reflect on how your thinking processes led you into giving the solution you came up with. If you got it correct, congratulations on not showing rigidity in your thinking and on avoiding a mental set. There are actually two other solutions to the third example, with the same area as the given solution. I will leave you to try to find these for yourself.

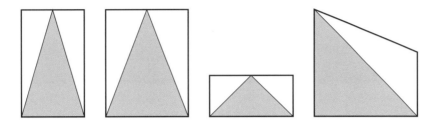

22.19: The parallelogram is as shown on the left below.

22.20: The parallelogram transforms into a rectangle of base 5 cm and height 3 cm, so the area is 15 cm².

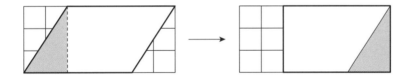

22.21: The area of the rectangle will be 60 cm². The triangles have areas of 10 cm² and 20 cm². So the area of the trapezium is 90 cm².

22.22: The area of the rectangle will be 60 cm². The two triangles will have a total area of 10 cm². So the area of the trapezium is 70 cm².

22.23: The area of the rectangle will be 130 cm². The two triangles will have a total area of 20 cm². So the area of the trapezium is 150 cm².

22.24: The area of a trapezium is the height multiplied by the mean of the lengths of the two parallel sides (half the sum of the lengths). This assumes that the two parallel sides are horizontal and the 'height' is the distance between them. Although we have used only simple examples to lead to this rule, it actually works for all trapeziums.

22.25: If the height of the box is 5 cm, the other two dimensions are 11 cm and 10 cm. The capacity of the box is 550 cm³.

22.26: If the height of the box is 6 cm, the other two dimensions are 9 cm and 9 cm. The capacity of the box is 486 cm³. It has decreased.

22.27: If $h = 4$ then the dimensions of the box are 4 cm, 11 cm and 13 cm. The capacity of the box is now 572 cm³.

22.28: In general, if the height is h cm, the other two dimensions are $(15 - h)$ cm and $(21 - 2h)$ cm.

22.29: The capacity of the box is found by multiplying these three together. We already have the results for $h = 6$, 5 and 4; these are entered in the table below, along with the results for $h = 3$.

h	$15 - h$	$21 - 2h$	Capacity (cm³)
6	9	9	486
5	10	11	550
4	11	13	572
3	12	15	540

It looks as though the maximum capacity might be somewhere between $h = 4$ and $h = 5$. So, try 4.5, 4.9, 4.1 and so on. You should find that the maximum capacity is achieved somewhere between $h = 4$ (capacity = 572 cm³) and $h = 4.1$ (capacity = 572.032 cm³).

22.30: The child has probably made the common error of counting the number of squares around the edge of the shape, rather than the actual edges of the squares that make up the perimeter. Discuss perimeter in terms of the length of fencing needed to go all the way around the edge of a field; or the path of an ant walking all the way round the edge of the shape.

22.31: The child may have mistaken perimeter for area, a common confusion when these two measures are taught simultaneously. It is more likely that the child is just responding to the numbers in the question and immediately sees the connection between 8 and 48 as $6 \times 8 = 48$. Challenge the error by asking the child to draw a rectangle 6 cm by 8 cm and find the perimeter. Use questions to clarify the distinction between area (the amount of space inside the rectangle) and perimeter (the distance around the edge).

22.32: The child has incorrectly applied the calculation of area for a rectangle (length × width) to the parallelogram. This is not surprising because teachers might sometimes say 'area equals length times width', without emphasizing strongly enough that this only applies to rectangles. A good starting point for clarifying this is for the child to make a rectangle 10 cm by 5 cm using four thin strips of card connected with paper fasteners, and then to gradually transform this into more and more oblique parallelograms (all 10 cm by 5 cm), noticing how the area clearly gets smaller and smaller.

22.33: You may have equally good but different ideas, but here is a possible sequence.

Question 2: What is the area in square units of triangle B?

Question 3: On the grid on the right, draw a rectangle with **double** the area of rectangle A.

Question 4: On the grid on the right, draw a rectangle with **half** the area of rectangle A.

Question 5: On the grid on the right, draw a triangle with **double** the area of triangle B.

22.34: Do the children confuse area with perimeter? (For example, giving 10 as the answer to question 1.)

Do they get in a muddle counting the fractions of squares in question 2?

Do they use the fact that 2 squares divided in half by a diagonal give an area of 1 square unit?

Do they use the idea that triangle B is half the area of a rectangle 4 units by 2 units?

Do they make the mistake of doubling the lengths to double the area? (For example, in question 3 drawing a rectangle with dimensions 6 units by 4 units.)

Do they double the areas of shapes A and B by doubling just the height or just the base? (Both are correct.)

Do they halve the areas of shapes A and B by halving just the height or just the base? (Both are correct.)

Does any child show a particularly creative (correct) response to any of these questions that could be shared with the class?

22.35: Here are two ideas: (i) Wrap a tape measure around the curved surface of the cylinder and read off the circumference; (ii) Put a mark on a point on a circular edge, then roll the cylinder along a non-slippery surface (mouse mats recommended) and measure how far it travels when the mark does a complete circuit.

22.36: Here are two suggestions: (i) Place a ruler across the circular top of the cylinder in such a way that produces the greatest possible distance from one point to the opposite point; measure this distance; (ii) Hold the cylinder in a vice (without squashing it) and measure the gap between the two sides of the vice.

22.37: The children should discover that the circumference of a circle divided by the length of the diameter is always just a bit more than 3. Rogue results that do not give a ratio in the range 3 to 3.3, say, can be checked and repeated if necessary. Children should learn some lessons about accuracy and approximation in measurement. The mean of all the results should be a fair approximation for the value of π. The teacher might explain to the children that if we could do the measurements really exactly, then this is the result we would get every time – and that what they have just discovered was known and used in various ancient civilizations.

22.38: (i) Just roll the card up into a cylindrical tube and glue the 2 cm flap against the opposite edge; (ii)–(iv) Score the card with dotted lines as shown below, fold along the scored lines and glue the flap against the opposite edge.

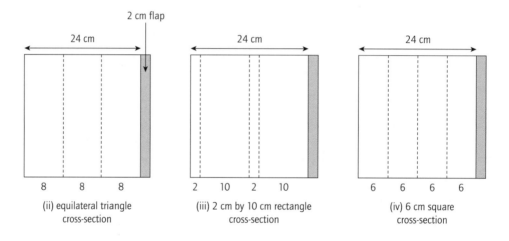

(ii) equilateral triangle cross-section   (iii) 2 cm by 10 cm rectangle cross-section   (iv) 6 cm square cross-section

22.39: In each case, the perimeter is 24 cm.

22.40: The child may be surprised to discover that the volume of sand varies from one shape to another, even though the same sheet of card was used and the perimeters of the cross-sections are all 24 cm. In order, from greatest to least volume, they should get the shapes with the following cross-sections: the circle, the square, the equilateral triangle, the rectangle 2 cm by 10 cm. Some children may be able to relate this result to the fact that a circle is the shape with the largest area for any given perimeter.

23.01: Sometimes the case. It is correct when both are clockwise or both anticlockwise; and not correct when one is clockwise and the other anticlockwise.

23.02: Always the case.

23.03: Always the case.

23.04: Sometimes the case. It is correct for a quadrilateral with angles of 110°, 110°, 70° and 70°; and incorrect for a quadrilateral with angles of 70°, 70°, 70° and 150°.

23.05: Never the case.

23.06: Never the case.

23.07: Sometimes the case. It is correct, for example, for a quadrilateral with angles of 10°, 10°, 100° and 240°; but it is incorrect for a quadrilateral with angles of 40°, 40°, 40° and 240°.

23.08: It also turns through an angle of 15°.

23.09: 180° ÷ 3 = 60°

23.10: 360° ÷ 4 = 90°

23.11: 540° ÷ 5 = 108°

23.12: 720° ÷ 6 = 120°

23.13: 900° ÷ 7 = 129° (approximately)

23.14: a = 130° (when added to the 50° it makes 180°)

23.15: c = 70° (it is vertically opposite to the given 70° angle). Then b and d both equal 110°.

23.16: $x + y$ = 360° − 200° = 160°. So each of x and y must equal 80°.

23.17: Internal angle R is equal to 180° − (55° + 38°), which is 87°. Subtracting the internal angles in turn from 180°, the external angles are 125° at P, 142° at Q and 93° at R.

23.18: The three external angles add up to a complete rotation, 360°.

23.19: Latitude is the angle turned through from the equator to the place in question. The North Pole is latitude 90°. So London to the North Pole requires a rotation through an angle of 90 − 51.5 = 38.5°.

23.20: The angle turned through would be 51.5 + 90 = 141.5°.

23.21: The sum of the angles in an n-sided polygon is $(2n − 4)$ right angles = $90(2n − 4)$ degrees. In a regular polygon, to find each of the angles we have to divide this by n. This gives: $[90(2n − 4) ÷ n]$ degrees as the size of each angle in an n-sided regular polygon.

23.22: The car has turned through 90° anticlockwise.

23.23: The car has turned through 90° clockwise.

23.24: The car has turned through 180° clockwise. A common error here is to say 360°. But that would leave you facing in the same direction as you did when you approached the roundabout, not the opposite direction.

23.25: The minute hand turns through 360° and the hour hand through 30°.

23.26: From noon to 12.30 p.m., the minute hand turns through 180° and the hour hand through 15°. So the angle between them is 165°.

23.27: In 30 minutes, the angle between the hands becomes 165°, which is 5.5° every minute. It will therefore take (90 ÷ 5.5) minutes for the hands to be at a right angle. That is about 16 minutes after noon. Also, the hands are at right angles when the angle between them is 270°. This takes 270 ÷ 5.5 = 49 minutes approximately after noon. So the hands are at right angles at about 12.16 p.m. and 12.49 p.m.

23.28: The correct observation is that b is greater than a. The child is misled because the lines for a are longer, and confuses the angle with the space between the lines. Emphasize the idea of 'difference in direction'. Extend the lines enclosing angle b and discuss whether or not the angle changes.

23.29: Angle c must equal 80°. Question the child to see if they are misapplying the idea that two angles on a line add up to 180°. Emphasize that the two parallel lines are in the same direction. For example, they are both heading due east.

23.30: This must be wrong because angle d is obtuse. The child has almost certainly used a protractor that shows both the obtuse and the acute angle here and read off the wrong angle. Show the angle as a rotation starting at zero degrees to the right on the protractor, noting when you pass 90°.

23.31: Turning a door handle. Opening a door. Rotating themselves to face the four walls in the classroom. Turning a page in a book. Turning the volume control up or down on some audio equipment. Flicking a rocker switch to turn a lamp on or off. And many more.

23.32: Give the children a sheet with four angles drawn on it, including a larger angle with quite short lines, and a smaller angle with quite long lines. Get the children to put them in order 'by eye'. Then ask them to cut them out and put them in order by placing one angle on top of another, with the vertices all coinciding. Then look through old magazines and find examples of angles. Draw lines on the pictures to show the angles clearly. Then again cut them out, compare them as before and make a display of angles from the pictures put in order from smallest to largest.

23.33: Ask two children to stand at the front of the class, with arms outstretched pointing forwards in the same direction. Tell them always to turn clockwise. Ask one child to turn to point at the door, and the other to turn to point at the middle of the back wall. Discuss who has turned through the greater or smaller angle. Repeat with lots of similar examples.

23.34: Here is one idea for a useful lesson. Quickly revise what are a right angle, a straight angle and a complete rotation in degrees. Display a carefully drawn angle (for example, 73°) and ask each child to write down an estimate for the size of the angle. By questioning, determine the smallest and largest estimate. Say these are 48° and 87°. Divide this range up into between five and ten subsets – for example, 46–50, 51–55, 56–60, 61–65, 66–70, 71–75, 76–80, 81–85 and 86–90. By a show of hands, ask how many estimates are in each category. Get the children to record these in a frequency table. Quickly produce a bar chart showing the distribution of estimates – this could be done on a computer, with the result immediately displayed on the interactive whiteboard. Discuss the distribution. Only now get some children to measure the angle and agree on its size. Now ask the question, how well did we do? Were most people in the 71–75 category? Talk about some familiar angles to use as reference items – such as 45° in a right-angled isosceles triangle, or 60° in an equilateral triangle. Then repeat with a different angle and see if the class does better this time. Extend to obtuse angles and even reflex angles.

24.01: True.

24.02: False (the term being defined is 'translation').

24.03: True.

24.04: True.

24.05: True.

24.06: False (scaling up requires a factor greater than 1, scaling down a factor less than 1).

24.07: True.

24.08: True.

24.09: False (it is a rotation).

24.10: True.

24.11: False (the figure shown, for example, has rotational symmetry of order 4, but no lines of symmetry).

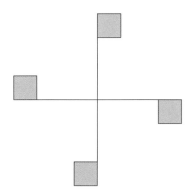

24.12: Shape X is transformed into shape A by a translation of 3 units to the right and 2 units down.

24.13: Shape A is transformed into shape X by a translation of 3 units to the left and 2 units up (the inverse of the transformation in 24.12).

24.14: Shape X is transformed into shape B by a rotation through 90° anticlockwise about the bottom left-hand corner of X.

24.15: Shape B is transformed into shape X by a rotation through 90° clockwise about the bottom right-hand corner of B (the inverse of the transformation in 24.14).

24.16: Shape X is transformed into shape C by a reflection in the horizontal line along the base of X.

24.17: Shape C is transformed into shape X by a reflection in the horizontal line along the base of X. (A reflection is always its own inverse.)

24.18: Shape P has reflective symmetry, with just one line of symmetry.

24.19: Shape Q has only rotational symmetry, of order 2.

24.20: Shape R has reflective symmetry, with four lines of symmetry. It also has rotational symmetry of order 4.

24.21: Here are some examples suggested by some mathematically creative Year 6 children:

They are both four-sided figures.

They both have four vertices labelled A, B, C and D.

They are both parallelograms.

They both have a diagonal line drawn from A to C.

They are both made up of five lines.

They both have opposite sides equal.

They both have opposite sides parallel.

They both have rotational symmetry of order 2.

They have the same area.

They have the same height.

They both are divided into two halves of the same area.

They both have no lines of symmetry.

24.22: The two reflections in the parallel mirror lines are equivalent to a translation of 10 units to the right.

24.23: Remarkably, this is the case wherever you put the object, if you first reflect it in A and then in B.

24.24: In general, the translation is always twice the distance between the parallel mirror lines.

24.25: Four sheets.

24.26: A scale factor of 2 (doubling all the lengths).

24.27: This would have to be a scaling which, when done twice, gives a scaling of 2. So it is the square root of 2, approximately 1.414.

24.28: A scale factor of 0.5.

24.29: The square root of 0.5, which is approximately 0.707.

24.30: The crucial point here is that, as we walk around our local space, left and right are not fixed, but they vary depending on which way you are looking. But up and down are fixed. If we face each other, your right is my left; but we both have the same up and the same down. So, left and right, and up and down are very different concepts. Teachers of young children, please note. Now, when I look in a vertical mirror and raise my left hand, the image in the mirror raises the hand that is on my left. But, in relation to the direction the image is facing, this is its right hand. But we have the same up and the same down, because these are invariant. If I point upwards, the image points upwards (albeit with an apparently different hand). Having said that, we can reverse top and bottom by standing on a mirror placed on the floor. Now my image is upside down with the feet above the head (at least in my world). A horizontal mirror turns the world upside down.

24.31: (a) a circle or any regular polygon; (b) a diamond shape, e.g. a quadrilateral with angles 60°, 100°, 100°, 100°; (c) a parallelogram that is not a rhombus; (d) a triangle with angles 90°, 30° and 60°.

24.32: You may have other ideas, but here are some of mine. One way is to draw round the shape to make a box into which it will fit; then pick the shape up and turn it over, thus producing its mirror image. If the shape has reflective symmetry, it will still fit into its box. A second way is to cut out the shape drawn on paper and see if it has any lines of symmetry, by folding. A third way is to place a mirror across the shape and see if there is a position in which the bit of the shape you can see and its image together make the original shape. Or you can draw round the shape on tracing paper, turn the paper over and see if the shape will fit into the mirror image showing through the paper.

24.33: Here are some suggestions, but maybe you have come up with some ideas better than these. A good way of testing for rotational symmetry is to draw round the shape to make a box into which it will fit. Then rotate the shape and see in how many different positions it will fit into its box. Another is to get two identical plastic shapes, place one on top of the other so they line up exactly and then put a mark in the same place on the edge of both shapes. Then rotate the top shape to see if there are any other positions in which they line up exactly, and mark the top shape immediately above the mark on the bottom shape. The number of marks you can make is the order of rotational symmetry.

24.34: Reflect the vertices first and then draw the lines. In a reflection, each point in the given shape is reflected onto its mirror image in the mirror line. So, first reflect each vertex of the quadrilateral onto its mirror image. So a point that is, for example, 4 units to the right of the mirror line is reflected onto a point 4 units to the left, moving along a line at right angles to the mirror line. When all the vertices have been reflected, connect them with straight lines to get the required mirror image.

24.35: Translate the vertices first and then draw the lines. A positive translation in the horizontal direction is to the right and a negative one is to the left. A positive translation in the vertical direction is up and a negative one is down. So translate each of the vertices here 2 units to the right and then 3 units down. When all the vertices have been translated, connect them with straight lines to get the required mirror image.

24.36: When you can see a square, the angle between the mirrors is 90°.

24.37: When you can see a regular hexagon, the angle between the mirrors is 60°.

24.38: The numbers of lines of symmetry in the sequence of shapes are 3 (for the equilateral triangle), 4 (for the square), 5 (for the regular pentagon), 6 (for the regular hexagon), 7 (for the regular heptagon) and so on.

24.39: Eventually, provided you have enough light to see it, the regular shape you can see has so many sides that it approximates to a circle – a shape with an infinite number of lines of symmetry.

25.01: True. A rhombus is a parallelogram with all four sides equal.

25.02: False. A square is a special rhombus with all four angles equal, as well as the four equal sides of a rhombus.

25.03: False. It could be an oblong rectangle.

25.04: True. An equilateral triangle is a special case of an isosceles triangle.

25.05: False. This would make the sum of the angles greater than 180°.

25.06: False. A square is a rectangle with all four sides equal.

25.07: True. Try it and see.

25.08: False. A regular hexagon will tessellate, but not all hexagons.

25.09: True. Each one passes through a vertex and the midpoint of the opposite side.

25.10: False. The word 'side' in geometry should be used only for the straight edges of polygons. A polygon with 10,000 sides, say, would look to us like a circle: theoretically, a circle can be thought of as a polygon with an infinite number of sides.

25.11: True. A regular tetrahedron has four faces, all equilateral triangles.

25.12: False. A cube is a cuboid with all the edges equal in length.

25.13: False. Only plane surfaces should be called 'faces'.

25.14: False. You need six square faces to make a cube; a square-based pyramid has only one.

25.15: True. It consists of two identical octagons joined by eight rectangular faces.

25.16: True. A regular dodecahedron has 12 faces, each of which is a regular pentagon, with 5 equal sides. $5 \times 12 = 60$; but each edge is shared by two faces, so 30 edges in total.

25.17: False. The word 'face' in geometry should be used only for flat (plane) surfaces, such as the faces of a polyhedron. A sphere does not have any faces; just one continuous curved surface.

25.18: American Samoa.

25.19: Malta, Monaco.

25.20: Czech Republic.

25.21: Republic of the Congo.

25.22–25.24: The shaded planes in the diagrams below show how the cuts might be made. Note that these are not the only ways of cutting off the required shapes.

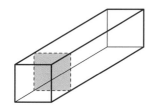 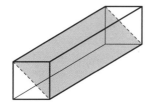 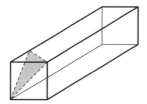

25.25: X is the net of a cuboid, 3 units long, 2 units wide and 1 unit high. Y is the net of a square-based pyramid with all edges equal in length. Z is the net of a prism with a cross-section that is a regular pentagon.

25.26: Figure Q is not the net of a cuboid.

25.27: You cannot do this unless the triangle you start with is obtuse-angled. Then just draw any line through one of the acute-angled vertices so that it cuts the opposite side of the triangle. The triangle is now divided into two obtuse-angled triangles. So, together with the original triangle, the diagram now contains three obtuse-angled triangles.

25.28: The first bit of creative thinking is to draw a quadrilateral that has a reflex angle, as shown below. The next bit is to recognize one triangle contained within another triangle.

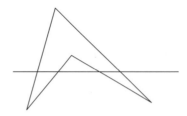

25.29: To make the third expansion, 12 grey tiles are added.

25.30: To make the fourth expansion, 16 black tiles are added.

25.31: $1 + 4 + 8 + 12 + 16 + 20 + 24 + 28 + 32 + 36 + 40 = 221$.

25.32: The total number of tiles is $2n(n + 1) + 1$. For example, for the second expansion $n = 2$; then this formula gives the total as $4(2 + 1) + 1$, which equals 13 tiles.

25.33: Turn the paper round and talk about what happens. Get the child to cut out the shape and put it on the desk. Compare it with plastic squares from the shape box. Put the plastic square on a piece of paper and rotate it slowly. Is it still a square? Get the child to draw round it. Ask the child what they notice.

25.34: Draw a circle on the sphere (largest possible). Draw round the edges of one of the faces of the cube to make a square. Copy the circle and square onto a piece of paper. Have a discussion about the difference between solid shapes (like spheres and cubes) and flat shapes drawn on a piece of paper (like circles and squares). Use various other examples of 2-D and 3-D shapes and ask the children whether they are solid shapes or flat shapes. Get the children to identify all the flat shapes making up a solid shape, like a triangular prism.

25.35: Ask the child to cut out several parallelograms and fold them along their diagonals. Do the two halves fold exactly one on top of the other? No! So, is it a line of symmetry? Also, draw round a plastic or card parallelogram, then turn it over and see if it will now fit in its box. Or place a mirror along the diagonal and look in the mirror. Is the shape you can see the original parallelogram?

25.36: The implication seems to be that rectangles are regular shapes, since the statement then goes on to talk about *irregular* shapes. Rectangles in general are not regular. The only rectangles that are regular are squares.

25.37: Ask these questions. Are all the edges the same length? Yes, OK so far. Are all the faces identical? Yes, OK so far. Are all the angles on each face the same? Yes, they are all 60°. Still OK! Does the same number of edges meet at each vertex? No, so for this reason it cannot be a regular polyhedron. (My thanks to a Norwich teacher, Jenny Ross-Nevin, for providing this example.)

25.38: At stage (i): what makes you think it might be a triangle? What kind of triangle would it be, if it were? At stage (ii): now, why have you changed your mind? What makes you think it might be a rectangle? What are these two angles? What would have to be hidden for this to be a rectangle? At stage (iii): now, why do you think it might be a square? Is a square a rectangle? In what way is a square a special rectangle? Could this shape still be something other than a square?

25.39: Almost any shape, particularly if their orientation is not as we usually see them in books.

25.40: The objective of this activity is to reinforce the children's knowledge and accurate use of the language required to describe the properties of familiar geometric shapes.

26.01: In a block graph, each column consists of a number of squares and the frequency represented by the column is given by counting the number of squares. It is not necessary therefore to have a vertical axis. However, in a bar chart it is the height of the column that represents the frequency. A vertical axis is required so that the frequency can be read from the scale on this axis.

26.02: A discrete variable can take only specific, separate values across a particular range, often (but not always) just whole number values. For example, the number of letters in a child's first name is a discrete variable. In a typical class of children, for example, this variable might take only whole number values from 2 to 11. A continuous variable can potentially take any value across a range, including all possible fractional or decimal values. For example, the height of a child is a continuous variable. As a child's height increases from, say, 152 cm to 153 cm, it moves continuously through all the possible heights between 152 cm and 153 cm: it does not suddenly go up in jumps from one value to the next.

26.03: There is actually very little difference between a simple pictogram and a block graph. In a simple pictogram, each item in the population is represented by an icon. The icons are arranged in an orderly manner in rows or columns, so that at a glance you can compare the relative frequencies in different subsets. A block graph is really just a pictogram that uses a square as the icon, joining the squares together to make a column.

26.04: The data is discrete. The only possible values of the variable are 64, 65, 66, 67 and so on, up to 312.

26.05: Because there are potentially so many different values for this discrete variable, it will be necessary to group the data, before representing it in a bar chart. One possibility would be to group the data using intervals of 50 pages: this produces six subsets (for example, 50–99, 100–149, 150–199, 200–249, 250–299, 300–349). Another would be to use intervals of 25 pages: this produces 11 subsets (for example, 50–74, 75–99, 100–124, 125–149, 150–174, 175–199, 200–224, 225–249, 250–274, 275–299, 300–324).

26.06: The completed tally chart is as shown:

Jan–Mar	卌 卌 卌 卌 卌 IIII
Apr–Jun	卌 卌 卌 卌 II
Jul–Sep	卌 卌 卌 卌 卌 III
Oct–Dec	卌 卌 卌 卌 I

26.07: The frequency table is as shown:

Quarter	Number of pupils
Jan–Mar	29
Apr–Jun	22
Jul–Sep	28
Oct–Dec	21

26.08: The bar chart is as shown:

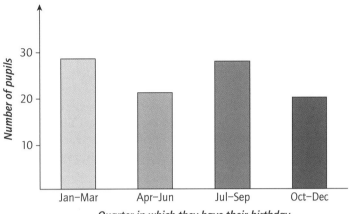

Quarter in which they have their birthday

26.09: A pie chart would be appropriate because the variable has only four values.

26.10: The 100 is $\frac{1}{3}$ of the population of 300, so the angle in the pie slice would be $\frac{1}{3}$ of 360°, which is 120°.

26.11: There are just far too many values of the variable for a pie chart to be used.

26.12: Because the variable is 'time', this data could be represented sensibly as a line graph, plotting the frequency for each month of each year.

26.13: At least the following:

- How were 'coffee lovers' identified?
- Did they ensure that the sample of the coffee lovers asked for their preference was random?
- What was the size of the sample that gave their opinions?
- 'Prefer their coffee' when compared to how many other and which other coffees?
- Did they include in their results those who expressed no preference?

I would not be impressed by this statistic if, for example, they identified 'coffee lovers' by asking people drinking coffee in one of their own coffee shops if they were coffee lovers. This would not be a random group. Nor would I be impressed if the sample was only 20 people; nor if they asked for a preference when compared with only one other brand; nor if they discounted those who gave no preference.

26.14: The bar chart 'suppresses zero'. By not drawing the vertical axis from zero, the impression is given of a much larger proportion in favour of the proposal than was the case: it looks like about 50% in the 'yes' column, when in fact it is only about 37.5%.

26.15: The total number of trainees was 5 + 12 + 42 + 23 + 8 = 90.

26.16: The number with 2 or more A levels was 73 out of 90. This is approximately 81.1%.

26.17: You might use, for example, an Excel spreadsheet, entering the data in two rows exactly as shown in the table. You should select the data for the numbers of trainees (5, 12, 42, 23, 8), then click on 'charts' and select the pie chart option like the one shown. You will need to find an option in the toolbox that puts the percentages into the slices of the pie. The final challenges will be to get the key alongside the chart to indicate the numbers of A levels (0, 1, 2, 3, 4) and then to insert a title for the chart. (This procedure may vary for different versions of the software.)

26.18: These are my examples of two possible questions: Have you ever been to Paris (P)? Have you ever been to Edinburgh (E)?

26.19: These divide the children into four subsets: those who have been to P and E; those who have been to P but not E; those who have been to E but not P; those who have been to neither P nor E.

26.20: These could be represented either in a Venn diagram with two overlapping sets (labelled P and E) or in a Carroll diagram (with the rows labelled P and not P, and the columns labelled E and not E).

26.21: This is data over time. It would therefore be appropriate to use it to develop skills in representing time-related data in a line graph. The horizontal axis will show the ages of children: 5 years, 6 years, 7 years and so on. Children could be shown how to mark points showing the percentages of children at these ages regularly cycling to school, and then to join the points with lines. Discuss with the children how the resulting graph gives an appropriate picture of how the variable changes with age, particularly focusing on the way the percentage increases.

26.22: This data could be used to show children how a continuous variable like 'distance' has to be rounded to the nearest something, in order to process it and represent it. The distance that children travel to school is theoretically a continuous variable. By rounding the distances to, say, the nearest kilometre, this makes it, in effect, a discrete variable. If the rounded distances range from 0 km to, say, no more than 10 km, then the data could be put directly into a bar chart, with the horizontal axis labelled 'distance travelled to school to the nearest km'. With primary children, it will be acceptable then to label the columns 0 km, 1 km, 2 km and so on. Because the original variable is continuous, I would incline towards drawing the columns of the bar chart without gaps. Ask children to make up questions that can be answered from their bar charts – and to answer each other's questions.

26.23: This discrete data could be represented in a bar chart, with a column for each of the different responses, with gaps between the columns. Because there is likely to be a small number of different responses (car, train, air, no preference), the data would be particularly appropriate for a pie chart. Children could learn how to enter the data into a spreadsheet and how to get the computer to generate a pie chart. Discuss with the children what is represented by the whole pie and by various slices of the pie.

26.24: You could ask the child to present the same data in a bar chart and then discuss the differences between the two. The most important question is, what do the lines joining up the points represent? In this case they do not represent anything. There is no gradual movement from, say, an apple to a plum. Compare examples where the horizontal axis represents time, in which case the line does represent a kind of gradual change over time. So, it is better with this data to use a picture that shows the different subsets as separate and unconnected.

26.25: A really important principle in using pie charts is that the whole pie must represent 100% of the population, in this case the 30 children in the class. This is not the case in the diagram shown. The reason for this is that some children have clearly visited more than one attraction. This data cannot be put into a pie chart.

26.26: There are five crosses in the cell for 1 girl and 1 boy, representing 5 families.

26.27: The four crosses in the top two rows show that there were 4 families with more than 2 boys.

26.28: 12 families had 2 children. That's 3 families with just 2 boys, 4 families with just 2 girls, and 5 families with one of each.

26.29: Here are just a few suggestions:

- How many families with no boys? (7)
- How many families with 2 girls? (10)
- How many families with the same number of girls as boys? (6)
- How many families with fewer girls than boys? (11)
- How many families with more than 2 children? (14)
- What is the most common type of family? (1 boy and 1 girl)
- What is the largest family? (2 girls, 4 boys)
- Why no crosses in the (0, 0) square? (Must be at least 1 child.)

26.30: Here are some suggestions. The children should be able to:

- decide when a set of data for a discrete numerical variable should be grouped into intervals for the purposes of drawing a bar chart;
- recognize that the intervals used for grouping should be equally sized;
- decide how best to group the data, in order to produce between 5 and 12 subsets;
- collect and correctly group a set of data into appropriately sized intervals;
- put the results into a frequency table;
- draw and label correctly the horizontal and vertical axes for the bar chart, using an appropriate scale for the vertical axis if the frequencies are large;
- accurately draw the columns for each subset, with gaps between them;
- as an alternative, enter the data from the frequency table into a spreadsheet and use this to generate an appropriate bar chart;
- correctly state what each column of the completed chart represents;
- make comparisons between the subsets using the completed chart and language such as more than, less than, greatest, least;
- interpret and answer questions about bar charts for grouped discrete data produced by other people.

27.01: There are 27 chapters in the book (the sum of the numbers in the second row of the table).

27.02: The total number of pages occupied by the 27 chapters is $(7 \times 1) + (8 \times 3) + (9 \times 2) + (10 \times 3)$ … and so on, which equals 322.

27.03: The mode is 13 pages per chapter (more of these than any other number of pages).

27.04: The minimum number of pages per chapter is 7.

27.05: The maximum number of pages per chapter is 18.

27.06: The range is 11 pages (the difference between the maximum and the minimum).

27.07: The median is 12 pages.

27.08: The mean is $322 \div 27$, which is about 11.9 pages.

27.09: The mean is about 12 pages and the median is 12 pages. The mode is 13 pages. So, a reasonable summary is: 'Typically there are about 12 or 13 pages per chapter.'

27.10: The scores of all 95 children in School A would have been listed in order from smallest to largest. The score in the middle (the 48th in the list) is the median score.

27.11: LQ and UQ are the lower quartile and the upper quartile. These would have been the scores one-quarter and three-quarters of the way along the list: the 24th and the 72nd in the list.

27.12: The top 25% of children in School B all scored 120 or more.

27.13: The bottom 25% of children in School B all scored 86 or less.

27.14: Their medians are very similar (102 and 101), but School B has a much larger interquartile range (120 − 86 = 34) than School A (112 − 92 = 20). This means that School B has a much wider spread of IQ scores than School A.

27.15: This tells you that 90% of the combined population scored from 81 to 124: all the children in School A are in this range. Anyone scoring less than 81 is in the bottom 5% of children on this test. Anyone scoring over 124 is in the top 5%. No children in School A were in either the bottom 5% or the top 5%. School B has the children with the lowest IQ scores and the children with the highest IQ scores.

27.16: For the bookshop, my estimates would be about 20%, 30% and 50% of R, E and F. These proportions give the estimated numbers of books sold as 80, 120 and 200 of R, E and F, respectively.

27.17: For the supermarket, I estimate that the proportions are about 10%, 20% and 70%, which indicate the number of books sold to be 25, 50 and 175 of R, E and F, respectively.

27.18: This must be true.

27.19: This must be true.

27.20: This is not necessarily true. It would be correct if all the classes were the same size. To convince yourself, take an extreme example: 98 children in the class with a mean age of 8.85 and 1 child in each of the other classes. The total of their ages would be (98 × 8.85) + 8.54 + 8.38 = 884.42; so the mean age would be about 8.84.

27.21: This is not necessarily true. Mean scores can be distorted by a few very large or very small items, so you cannot assume an even distribution of ages across the range.

27.22: The mean is 11 (55 ÷ 5) and the median is also 11 (the middle number in the sequence).

27.23: The mean is 14.5 (87 ÷ 6) and the median is also 14.5 (halfway between 13 and 16).

27.24: The mean and the median are always equal. The main point of this task is the process rather than the actual result.

27.25: 10 hours.

27.26: 8 hours.

27.27: The whole journey of 800 miles takes 18 hours, so the average speed is about 44.4 miles per hour (800 ÷ 18). Note that this is less than the mean of the outward average speed and the return average speed (45 miles per hour). Some people are surprised to discover this. The reason is that the outward journey takes longer and so the slower speed has a greater effect on the mean speed.

27.28: The answer is NOT 60 miles per hour. In fact, having completed the first 100 miles at an average of 20 miles per hour, it is then impossible to achieve an overall average of 40 miles per hour. A total of 200 miles at an average of 40 miles per hour takes 5 hours. But 100 miles at an average of 20 miles per hour takes 5 hours, so I have already used up all the time available on the outward journey. I would have to travel back at infinite speed and get home 'in no time at all'.

27.29: The mode is 3.

27.30: The range is 5.

27.31: Why use an entirely abstract set of numbers to test statistical understanding, which can and should be experienced in real-life contexts? For what possible purpose might anyone want to know the range and mode of a set of context-free numbers? In Question 27.29 it is bad mathematics to use the mode as a representative figure for a set as small as this. Question 27.30 is a fairly pointless question, assessing only whether the child remembers that in data-handling we use the word 'range' to mean the difference between the maximum and minimum value. The answer 'from 3 to 8' would be marked wrong, although the child giving this answer has not shown any significant misunderstanding. Mode and range do not go well together as statistics. Range and median are a more usual combination.

27.32: The first question to discuss is whether they collect data for all the Year 6 children in the two schools or use samples. For this level of mathematics, it would probably be best to collect data from two samples of the same size (such as 40 children in each school), so that actual numbers can be compared rather than proportions. Then discuss how to choose the samples – the first 40 children in alphabetical order would be OK. Then help the children to construct a simple questionnaire to be completed on a given date: (a) How did you travel to school today? [Choose from: bus, bike, car, walk]; (b) About how many minutes did it take you? The data for (a) is organized directly into four discrete subsets ready for representation in a graph. The data for (b) will have to be grouped appropriately – for example, 1–5, 6–10, 11–15 and so on.

27.33: For the data in (a) the mode would be a useful average to use, comparing the most common ways of getting to school. To compare the two schools for the data in (b), it would be very easy and appropriate to use the range as a measure of spread and the median as an average journey time.

27.34: The diagrams that follow are examples of how the two sets of data for each question could be represented for comparison, although these are not the only ways of doing this.

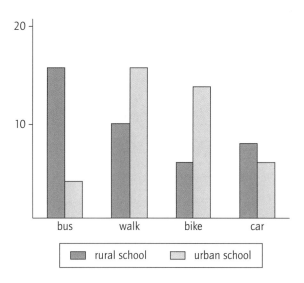

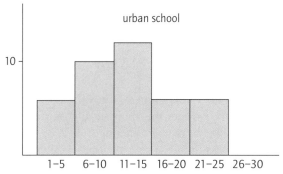

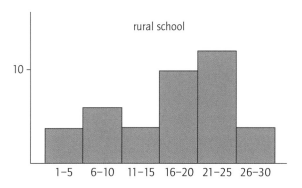

27.35: Test A, with a median score of about 68, looks harder than Test B, with a median score of about 80. The lowest mark on Test A was quite a lot lower than that on Test B. Someone managed to get everything correct in Test B, but not in Test A.

27.36: Test A has a greater spread, so it discriminates more between children. Test A might be the better test for summative assessment purposes, but half the children are getting about a third of the test wrong, which is discouraging for them. Test B would be better than Test A if the teacher wanted to encourage children by showing them what they can do: half the children get 80% or more and the top quarter of the children are scoring 90–100%. Even the lowest-scoring child gets a score of 58%.

28.01: It is just as likely to happen as not to happen.

28.02: This is a judgement that the event will never happen.

28.03: My example is: 'The total score is less than 3.'

28.04: It is bound to happen.

28.05: One example is: 'The total score is less than 19.'

28.06: My suggestions: highly unlikely, fairly unlikely, fairly likely, highly likely.

28.07: Go through all the records and find the proportion of test matches at the Oval in which the side batting last has scored 500 or more to win the match. If it has never been done then we would have to assign a probability of zero. But, interestingly, we would not want to say that it is impossible or that it should never happen.

28.08: In this case, we could do an experiment, throwing a die a large number of times. But it is better to consider this theoretically on the basis of symmetry. There are six equally likely possible outcomes (1, 2, 3, 4, 5, 6) of which four (1, 2, 3, 4) are scores less than 5. The probability is therefore $^4/_6$ or $^2/_3$.

28.09: This will require a survey. Select an appropriate sample of people, ask each one to choose a number less than 10 and record the answers. The proportion choosing 7 is an estimate of the probability required. The larger the sample the better, but I would suggest that a few hundred would be sufficient to identify a significant trend.

28.10: H1, H2, H3, H4, H5, H6, T1, T2, T3, T4, T5, T6.

28.11: There are 12 possible outcomes of which T3 is one so the probability of getting T3 is $^1/_{12}$ or approximately 0.083 (to 3 decimal places).

28.12: 3 in 12, so the probability is $^1/_4$ or 0.25.

28.13: Again, 3 in 12, so the probability is $^1/_4$ or 0.25.

28.14: Yes, they are. It is not possible for both events to occur simultaneously.

28.15: This occurs in 6 of the 12 outcomes, so the probability is $^1/_2$ or 0.5. This is the sum of the answers in Questions 28.12 and 28.13, because the events in those two questions are mutually exclusive.

28.16: 4 in 12, so the probability is $^1/_3$.

28.17: This occurs in 5 of the 12 outcomes (T1, T2, T3, T4, T6), so the probability is $^5/_{12}$.

28.18: This is because the two events in Questions 28.12 and 28.16 are not mutually exclusive.

28.19: $^1/_3$.

28.20: Yes.

28.21: Because the outcomes of each throw are independent, we can multiply the probabilities of each die showing yellow: $^1/_3 \times ^1/_3 = ^1/_9$.

28.22: The probability of all six showing yellow is $^1/_3 \times ^1/_3 \times ^1/_3 \times ^1/_3 \times ^1/_3 \times ^1/_3 = ^1/_{729}$, which is about 0.0014; in other words, extremely unlikely.

28.23: Because each throw is independent of what has happened in previous throws, even if yellow has come up 10 times in succession, the probability of yellow next time is still $^1/_3$.

28.24: Counter-intuitively, this outcome is very likely to occur. The probability is actually greater than 0.95. You will have to trust me on this, because the mathematics is tricky. But try it a few times when you're next in the library and you may be convinced.

28.25: The probability of getting two spades in succession is $^1/_4 \times ^1/_4 = ^1/_{16}$, which is about 0.06. I'm already sceptical. The probability of three spades in succession is $^1/_4 \times ^1/_4 \times ^1/_4 = ^1/_{64}$, which is about 0.016. That's unlikely enough for me – they're cheating!

28.26: They are all equally likely. Honest!

28.27: These events are not independent. Clearly, being alive at 80 is dependent on being alive at 70.

28.28: Nor are they mutually exclusive, since both can happen to the one person.

28.29: If both events occur then the person concerned will be alive at 80. The probability of both events occurring is therefore the same as the probability of being alive at 80, which is 0.5.

28.30: I don't have much idea what this might mean – but this is typical of the way statistics are used in advertising and politics to give an impression of confidence in a product or argument. First, it all depends on what is being increased. Does it refer to your chances of losing weight on some alternative slimming programme? Or to your chances of losing weight if you do nothing? Second, what is a 50% increase in the chances? If I start with a probability of 0.2 and increase this by 50% does this go up to 0.7 (increasing the probability by 0.5) or to 0.3? Third, what counts as losing weight? And, how did they arrive at this statistic anyway?

28.31: Ask what are all the possible scores, namely 2 to 12. The number they should expect to occur most often is 7. This is because there are more ways of scoring 7 (1 and 6, 2 and 5, 3 and 4, 4 and 3, 5 and 2, 6 and 1) than any other number from 2 to 12. Make sure the children understand that '1 and 6' and '6 and 1' have to be counted as different outcomes. Also stress that some other number might actually occur more often; the theory just tells us that this is unlikely if we have a large sample of throws of the dice.

28.32: The two numbers that they should expect to occur least often are 2 and 12. Explain that this is because there is only one way of scoring each of these numbers (1 and 1, 6 and 6). Again, stress that we are talking about what is likely to happen, not what must happen. That's the nature of probability.

28.33: This approach gives a good-sized sample of 600 results, enough to give reasonable estimates of the probabilities for each score. Here's how I suggest you might use the data. Aggregate all the frequencies into one frequency table. Ask the class to divide each frequency by 600 to obtain an estimate for each probability. For example, if 11 comes up 32 times, an estimate for the probability of scoring 11 is $32 \div 600 = 0.05$ (two decimal places is sufficient). These experimental probabilities can then be displayed in a graph. The children could then discuss the shape and the approximate symmetry of the graph, noticing that the probabilities increase for scores from 2 to 7 and then reduce for 7 to 12 (at least that is what you would expect to happen). The class may then be able to compile a two-way table (6 rows by 6 columns) to show all the possible scores for the two dice, use this to determine theoretical probabilities (the probability of scoring 7, for example, is $^{6}/_{36}$ or $^{1}/_{6}$) and then compare these with the experimental ones. Stress that the probabilities do not predict exactly what will happen, they just tell us how likely it is.

28.34: To collect data to assess the probability of this event occurring, ask a small group of children to do a survey of, say, a sample of 200 children in total and to record how many times the reply is 'carrot'.

28.35: To collect data to assess the probability of this event occurring, ask children in pairs to throw three dice 25 times and to record how many times they get two of the three numbers the same. Aggregate the results for the whole class to get a large sample.

28.36: To collect data to assess the probability of this event occurring, ask children in pairs to open books at 25 different pages randomly and to record how many times the first word is 'the'. Aggregate the results for the whole class to get a large sample.

28.37: To collect data to assess the probability of this event occurring, get each child in the class to play ten rounds of the game with three different people (outside of the class) using the strategy given, and then to report how many times they win more rounds than they lose. Again, aggregate the results for the whole class to get a large sample.

28.38: Before collecting data, get the children to talk about how likely they feel these events are. Ask them to compare various pairs of the events in terms of which of the two is more or less likely. Ask them to put the four events in order from the least likely to the most likely, using their intuition. Get the children subjectively to give each event a score out of 100, where 0 means they think it will never happen, 50 means evens and 100 means they think it is certain to happen. Then collect the data by experiment or survey for reasonably large samples, as appropriate (see notes on Questions 28.34–37). Once the data is collected, use this to estimate probabilities. Compare the intuitive assessments. Discuss at length. Have a great mathematical experience!